A LIFETIME OF CHANCES

by
Mary Chance VanScyoc

A LIFETIME OF CHANCES

by
Mary Chance VanScyoc

Printed in the United States of America
by Wichita Press, affiliate of Chance Industries
ISBN 0-9649065-0-3

Published by Parkwood Press
P.O. Box 20550, Wichita, Kansas 67208-1550

In loving memory of
my parents, sister, husband and son.

Thanks to my daughters, Betty Carson and Martha Shaw, who have been so supportive. I would have given up many times without them. And to Judy Rombold, my editor, chief tweaker, mentor, friend and so much more. Without her help and encouragement, this book would not have been published. And to Bill Carroll and Richard Holmes for their helpful comments and suggestions.

And, finally, thanks to all those wonderful people, named or unnamed, who crossed my path and who provided many of the stories in this book.

TABLE OF CONTENTS

PROLOGUE

Born in Wichita, Kansas, Mary Chance VanScyoc is a self-confessed tomboy, an athlete, a teacher, one of the country's first female air traffic controllers and a multi-rated pilot who learned to fly a helicopter at the age of 64. Her active, questing spirit comes naturally for she is from a family of adventurers.

Her great-grandparents emigrated from Norway, sailing steerage, and worked their way to the rugged Midwest. Another set of great-grandparents were Kansas pioneers, battling grasshopper plagues and hiding in the tall corn when Indians were near. Her brother founded a highly successful company that designs and makes carnival rides. And her father was a free spirit who could not be contained. He built, repaired and rebuilt almost anything mechanical, raced and jumped motorboats over ramps (even though he could not swim), raced cars and motorcycles and taught his family to challenge themselves at all times. Only Mary's mother led a more settled life, calmly adjusting to the whirl of activities going on about her, all the while holding the family together with loving care.

Mary's life has been a rich one; rich in spirit and challenge. Let her now tell of her family's and her own adventures.

WALSTAD AND BOGGESS GRANDPARENTS

Not only did I have adventurous parents, my grandparents and great-grandparents also were of sturdy stock. Mother's grandparents, Christian Jacob and Marian Anderson Walstad, were married in 1864 in the town of Christiana (now Oslo), Norway. Christian Jacob, my great-grandfather, said his father married the daughter of King Christian the Ninth, king of Norway and Sweden. He said his mother was disinherited for marrying a commoner. If this is correct, we all claim to be Norwegian royalty.

Great-grandpa Walstad had been a farmer in Norway in the 1860s and all they could ever have were the things the ground would produce for them. In those days, a man might earn 12 cents a day if he labored from 5 a.m. to 9 p.m. Their dream was to go to America, the land of opportunity, but he realized that he could not earn enough in years to buy passage for his wife and four children. (The third of these children was Helen, my grandmother, who was born in 1868.)

In 1870 Great-grandpa hired on as a sailor to the master of a sailing vessel. For wages, he was given passage from Christiana, Norway to New York. After nine weeks of squalls, icy water and storms he finally arrived in the New World.

He immediately boarded a train for Iowa, where there was a colony of Norwegian immigrants, and was hired by a cattleman. His job was to feed the cattle and in a year's time he had saved enough money, $200, to send for his family. One freezing day in October, 1871, Grandma Walstad, then 24 years old, walked up the gangplank of a steamer at Christiana and said good-bye to Norway. With her were her four children. Jacob, the oldest, was about six, Martin was five, Helen (my grandmother) was three, and Marta was one year old.

9

What a trip it must have been. Can you imagine starting out on such a voyage with four young children? Most of us don't even venture a trip to the grocery store with young children unless we have to. She and the four youngsters sailed to the United States as steerage passengers. The first time the weather permitted them to come up on deck, little Jacob nearly lost his life. A sudden squall blew up, sending a large wave sweeping over the deck that almost swept Jacob over the side. A man caught the youngster just in time to save him.

The rest of the voyage they remained below, warm enough but seasick. Grandma did not know one word of English and was worried about Martin, who had always been sickly. She did have, though, a piece of paper on which was written her husband's address. This bit of paper never left her person, and it finally brought her to her husband in Iowa. She was quoted in a newspaper interview at age 83 as saying, "Of course I wasn't scared. Never had enough sense to be scared."

But Grandma's troubles really began with the end of the voyage. The ship was due to land at New York, but the harbor was ice-locked, forcing the vessel to sail on to Boston. There they disembarked and the steamship company transported the immigrants from Boston to New York in the unheated cars of a freight train. There were large holes in the cars through which the freezing wind whistled. Grandma said it was all she could do to keep the children from falling through the holes. With all this little Martin caught a miserable cold.

After a long train trip they arrived at the Iowa town, then on the frontier, only to find that her husband was not there to meet her. Busy with feeding cattle, he had sent a cowboy with a wagon drawn by a team of mules. A frigid ride of 14 miles lay between the station and their new home, a one-room house with a bed or two and a cook stove. While waiting for her husband to finish his chores, Grandma hurriedly built a fire. It was too little and too late, however, to keep little Martin's cold from getting worse. He died two weeks later.

However, on that 14-mile trip, she saw two things she had never seen before — a cowboy and two mules. "We didn't have such brutes back in Norway," she said. There a farmer had only one horse. She never liked mules after that ride.

The family lived in Iowa until 1878, when they moved to Medicine Lodge, Kansas, traveling in a wagon and a hack. They took their cattle with them and filed papers on the land. By now they had six children and then had three more while living in Kansas, for a total of nine living after Martin's death. They soon needed more land for their stock so loaded up the wagon and hack in 1886 and drove 150 head of cattle about 200 miles across the plains from Medicine Lodge to Pampas, Texas. There they settled down for the rest of their lives.

Grandpa Walstad died in 1891 and Grandma in 1937 at age 89. I remember Grandma on several of her visits to Kansas. Her daughter, Blanche, usually came with her. I remember Aunt Blanche as being very crippled with arthritis and Grandma as a small lady (less than five feet tall) and very pleasant.

It was said that Grandma Walstad never used the word "hardship." She called it LIFE. When I find myself complaining about little inconveniences or discomforts, I try to think of my great-grandmother and all the hardships she survived. I take my hat off to the Walstads and all others who have endured so much to be a part of America.

I doubt that my grandmother (Helen) thought of it as enduring, but for the most part enjoyed the big adventure. She married Samuel Boggess (pronounced BOG-es) in 1886 at Medicine Lodge. I don't know anything about their courtship but Grandpa Samuel was in the grocery business all his life. They had seven children between 1887 and 1905: Ernest, Edna, Robert, Edith, Leona, Lois, and Florence. My mother, Lois, was born in 1899.

I have many memories of my Boggess grandparents, who lived in the Riverside area of Wichita. They had an old Model T with a door in the middle. We rode to the Baptist church in that unique car many times. They had a cherry tree in their back yard, which we loved to climb to pick (and eat) the cherries. Grandma always had a good stock of cookies. Sometimes she got them at the broken-cookie factory and sometimes a man came around with a basket of bakery products and she picked out goodies from him.

We always had our Thanksgiving dinners at their house. They had a long table that spread from the living room through the dining room. There were probably 25 of us there most of the time. I especially remember the pumpkin pie with nuts and whipped cream. My dad was pretty bored with the men in the Boggess family, so Thanksgiving is about the only time he went there. He would rather have been tinkering with machinery and I'm sure they weren't interested in that.

Grandpa Boggess was a pleasant man to be around and we all loved him. I think Grandma, however, was the dominant personality in that family. She seemed a little bossy to me, but I'm sure the family needed a boss. She was very kind and cared deeply for all her family. She, like many of her children, lost her mental faculties before she failed physically. She died in 1954 in Wichita at age 86. Grandpa had died in 1936.

Just a word about Mom's brothers and sisters. Ernest left home while Mother was very young so she hardly knew him. He was known as Whitey and moved to the Big Horn country of Montana near Lodge Grass. What I remember most about him is the fact that he was a bachelor until he was 40 years old, yet ended up having 18 children and step-children. He married Viola Green who had three children from a previous marriage. Together, they had three more children. She died in 1929 and Whitey married Margaret Mullenberg, who was a full-blooded Indian. They had three children together to add to the nine that Margaret had from a previous marriage. There was probably not a more beloved father than Ernest.

An article published in the Lodge Grass, Montana, paper at the time of his death in 1961 tells his story very well:

Ernest (Whitey) Boggess came to Big Horn country way back in 1908 to build the Big Horn dam, and died here Saturday at the age of 73 without seeing the start of construction on the project, which has been re-named Yellowtail. But Whitey was a builder, and when plans for the dam failed to materialize, he began work on road construction. Some of those early roads are still in use. His son, Ernest Jr., employed by the county road department, is currently repairing some of the roads his father built 50 years ago. Some are still in good condition and being traveled today. Even if Whitey didn't live to see construction on the dam actually begun, he did live long enough to see the letting of some of the preliminary work.

He was offered a job constructing the Big Horn dam in 1903, but when he arrived in this area he found plans for the dam had been canceled. But roads were needed, so Whitey got equipment and started to make traveling a little easier. Besides roads, he also constructed irrigation ditches and bridges. At first, most of the materials for the bridges were freighted in by wagon train. In 1920, the pioneer road builder decided to change his business and began farming in the Wolf Mountain area. Later he moved to the Good Luck Chicken Crossing region of Lodge Grass creek and there he farmed for 24 years. Ill health caused his retirement in 1954 and he made his home in Lodge Grass until last year, when he moved to Hardin. He served as a soldier during World War 1. He was buried in Custer Battlefield National Cemetery with military rites.

Edna was the second child and she was married to Homer Priest. They had three boys and a girl and lived in the desert east of Santa Barbara, California, all their married lives. I didn't see much of her, but when I saw her as an older woman, she was the very image of Grandma Helen Boggess. They lived in a rather crude dwelling on the desert. Homer wasn't too ambitious but I think that suited Edna fine. She died in California in 1963 at age 74.

Robert (Uncle Bob) was third. He had three wives, divorcing two of them. He had no children of his own but enjoyed his ex-wives' children. He always saw that his ex-wives were taken care of and supported his second wife until her death. We always enjoyed him as he was very fun-loving. He remained very close to all his sisters. He lived in Denver most of his life, but in later years moved with wife number three to California, where he died in 1979 at age 88.

Edith was married to Oscar Anderson and had a son, Donald. In 1930, when Donald was three years old and Edith was 35, she died giving birth to a daughter, named Dorothy. Grandma and Grandpa Boggess then took Oscar and his children into their home. Grandma had been keeping another grandson, Sammy Maxwell (son of Florence), when this happened so Sammy came to live with us part time while his mother worked. Grandma kept Oscar and his kids until he remarried and moved to Tulsa while the children were very young. Their stepmother, Marie (the only mother they ever knew), did a good job raising them. She is still living in a nursing home in Oklahoma.

Leona, the fifth child, married Clifford Schmidt in 1924. Cliff served in World War I and was in the banking and grocery business during their marriage. She worked in the insurance business until she retired. They had no children and the two of them were almost inseparable. He even went to the ladies' meetings with her. She was very much in love with him and when he said "jump" she asked, "How high?" They loved to travel, especially to Colorado. She is pictured in her jodhpurs riding horses, camping, and enjoying the outdoor life. She always had a smile on her face and was very good to her sisters, mother and nieces. She was almost a Pollyanna — nothing seemed to bother her. She died in 1978 at age 81 in Wichita.

Mother, Lois, was the sixth child. She and Leona were quite a bit alike, even though their husbands were not. The men tolerated each other, but both were very strong-minded characters. I will devote more space to Mother later as she was a very important part of my life.

Florence was the baby of the family and was a bit spoiled by these older sisters. She was impish and full of fun. We loved going to her house while we were growing up as she never let household chores stop her from playing games with us. She married Deacon Lowe and they had a son, Sammy. They divorced and she later married Wayne Maxwell. Wayne adopted Sammy and changed the boy's last name to Maxwell. He and Florence had a son, Wayne, Jr. They both worked for Western Union for many years and retired from there. Florence died in 1988 at age 83 in her home in Wichita.

Mother was the last surviving member of this family. She reigned over the Boggess family and was also the oldest member of the Chance family when she died in 1991. She always let us know she was "queen bee," in a fun way, and enjoyed her status to the fullest.

14

CHANCE GRANDPARENTS

My great-grandfather on Dad's side (we all called him Grandpa) was Nathan Chance, known as Nate. He was born in Grant County, Indiana in 1844. Grandma, Mary Emma (Em) McKnight, was born in 1843 in Bethesda, Ohio.

Grandpa was a Civil War veteran who fought with the 46th Iowa Infantry and was mustered out in Davenport, Iowa, at the close of the war. At the time of his death he was one of the last five Union Army survivors living in the Wichita area.

Grandma told me that they were married in Sheridan, Iowa, before church on Sunday morning the day before Christmas, 1865. After the simple ceremony, they attended services in the little frame country church, then went home and cooked their wedding dinner.

In 1874, they traveled to Kansas in a covered wagon and endured many hardships along the way. Their baby developed whooping cough, a very serious disease in those days as there was no treatment for it, but young Charlie survived. The family bought 160 acres just east of Wichita in Butler County for $1,000. The sod on this land still has never been broken.

Grandpa related that they moved to Kansas the same year the grasshoppers did. He said they didn't have much when they came but had a lot less after the grasshoppers left. Grandma had vivid recollections of the grasshopper plague and said she used to take her two little boys and hide in the corn fields when Grandpa went to town, so the Indians couldn't find them. After the grasshoppers' visit, though, there wasn't any corn to hide in.

Despite their hardships, Grandpa became a successful farmer and cattle rancher. Later they moved to Augusta, about five miles northeast of their farm, where they built one of the most imposing homes in that city. They lived there for 16 years before moving to a nice frame house in the east part of Wichita, where they lived until their deaths in 1940.

When I knew them best they were in their 80s and seemed ancient. Neither could see very well and Grandma was quite hard of hearing. They didn't even play the radio as they couldn't hear well enough to understand it, which made them nervous. They did have an Edison phonograph that we would play when we visited them. Grandpa worked in his garden well into his nineties and I suppose Grandma just took care of the house.

They lived only a block from their church and were quite faithful because by this time Grandpa had given up driving and the church was the focal point of their social life. They were 96 and 97 when they died and lacked about five months of being married 75 years. They were a grand old couple who lived and were happy in the days before inside toilets, electricity, running water or modern heating, and who made their own entertainment.

They had two boys, Charles and McKlveen (pronounced MAC-il-vane — what a name to give to a kid). Mac Chance, as he was known, was my grandfather. He was born in 1867 and in 1890 married Martha Holmes (known as Matt) in Benedict, Nebraska. Grandpa Mac was a pharmacist in Augusta where he was a charter member of the Augusta Christian Church and the church's first Sunday School superintendent. My children grew up in this church and I still have my membership there. In 1905 Grandma and Grandpa moved to Wichita and Grandpa traveled for a pharmaceutical company until he became ill. He died in 1916 when he was only 48 so I know very little about him.

Grandma was also very involved with the Christian Church. She was especially interested in the missionaries and was president of the Missionary Society of the Central Christian Church in Wichita for 25 years. She knew each of the church's missionaries personally. She also had a hand in choosing each minister and had strong opinions on the affairs of the church. The church was usually the topic of conversation when we visited her. Grandma was a kind lady, tall, with straight posture and a self-assured way about her. By the time I knew her she had endured the loss of a daughter, a husband, and a son. My father was her only direct heir and his children were her only grandchildren, so we always felt very special.

Grandmother always greeted us with a smile and never acted as though we were interrupting her. She loved the little ones as they came along and had a box of toys for them to play with. She always had beautiful flower gardens that she cared for in her back yard. I particularly remember the four o'clocks and Johnny-jump-ups — probably because they had odd names. We sat on her front porch swing or played a lot in Hyde Park across the street. We also slid down the cellar door and sometimes down the banister in the hallway — when she wasn't looking.

She tried everything she had an opportunity to do, saying she might not have a chance to pass that way again. When she was about 80 years old, hula hoops were all the rage so she tried one and did better than I did. She was a great fan of Charles Lindbergh, even naming her two canaries Lindy and Anne, and always said she would never fly with anyone else. But she did fly with me after I got my pilot's license.

Grandma owned a Cadillac until she bought a new 1929 Model A Ford, which she drove until about two months before her death in 1961. We always teased her about driving it 35 miles an hour, in town and on the highway. She drove too fast in town and too slowly on the highway but she never had a wreck that I'm aware of. She only drove it as far as El Dorado (35 miles) to visit her sister and to the Augusta cemetery (20 miles). Once when she was about 90, she was stopped by a policeman and refused to give her age, other than "legal."

Grandma wasn't wealthy but knew how to manage her money. She rented out rooms and apartments in her house since I can remember. One lady rented the sleeping room upstairs for many years. Grandma didn't live lavishly, but the things she bought were very nice. She had Persian rugs on the floors, Haviland china, wax fruit on the table, wicker furniture, and unusual parrot lamps. I'm sure she helped our family through some lean times when Mom and Dad were getting started at a young age. I think she bought houses for us to live in on several occasions.

17

In later years, Grandma decided she'd rather be called Granny. This was because by that time my mom, who was quite short, was also a grandmother and we called her "Little Grandma." Grandma Chance, who was quite tall, was "Big Grandma." Somehow "Granny" sounded better to her.

My sister, Geraldine, was her favorite grandchild, partly because she was the first grandchild and also because she liked going over there. Geraldine was always what I called a "sissy" and enjoyed dressing up and playing with dolls. Grandma would take her to nice places to eat and to shop and buy her clothes. They became very close as the years passed.

Granny taught me to embroider and, hoping to make me more lady-like, would often pay me for making a tea towel or a pillow slip. I would whip it up and then be out climbing trees again. She finally gave up. I loved Granny but was always busy being a tomboy. You can see why she and Geraldine got along so well.

We always spent the night at Granny's on the night before Christmas. I remember imagining we heard Santa outside and going to the window several times before finally falling asleep and missing his arrival. We had a lovely dinner on Christmas day with all the good china and silver, turkey, carrot and cheese casserole, and pie. She never even let us clear the table as I'm sure she didn't want us to break her good dishes. That was OK with us.

While they lived in Augusta, Grandma and Grandpa bought a Story and Clark upright piano, which was delivered by horse and buggy. When they moved to Wichita, it sat in their living room in one spot throughout her life. All the kids through the years played this piano, even if it was just a ditty. My dad's favorite piece was "Go tell Aunt Roatie." My daughter Martha has had this piano since 1973.

Grandpa and Grandma had three children. The first, Harold Winston, was born in 1891. The second was Fern, a beautiful little girl who was born in 1894 and died in 1896 at the age of 22 months. I do not know the cause of her death, but children's deaths were not uncommon in those days. She also is buried in Augusta. The last was Gerald, my dad.

Harold seemed to do everything right. He was a graduate of Fairmount University (now Wichita State University), an outstanding student and captain of the football team and was engaged to a fine lady when he joined the Army after graduation. He was a lieutenant and served in France in World War I. He was impatiently awaiting his time to return home after the armistice when he was stricken with meningitis and died in February 1919.

We have all the letters he wrote to his mother while in France. After reading them, I had a different view of Harold's personality. He also loved the adventurous life, had no use for the slackers and was a patriotic and caring person. He desperately wanted to go to the trenches but was assigned to be a machine gun instructor. He hated the mail service in France, loved the beauty of the country, worried about his mother being lonely and was sorry she had to worry about him. He knew a lot about the war and why they were fighting. He said many times that if we didn't really finish off the Germans, we would have it to do over again. How right he was.

One particular letter told how the French celebrated our Fourth of July holiday. He mentioned especially that nearly every house and business displayed an American flag, or other flags if they couldn't find an American flag. Then there were the activities of the day, which I will let him describe:

> I'll swear the entire town proceeded to the parade ground of the US Infantry where the track meet and ball games were held. Counting the soldiers, there must have been five thousand people there. Of course, Yanks predominated, then the French civilians, young and old, male and female, the maimed, the halt, and the blind, some British Tommies and French Poilus and here and there an American Negro soldier and now and then an Algerian in turban or fez.
>
> Now you know that France is not an athletic nation in any such sense as we are. Nine-tenths of these

people never saw a track meet and couldn't tell a ball game from a mob-scene in a "meller drama." So they got very much in the way, talked and gesticulated freely (a mild term) thoroughly enjoying the track meet and really GOT most of it. But when the ball game started, well you would have to see it to appreciate it. At first they wanted to sit out on the field. Our French mayor and a French captain carried a bench out and planted it about twenty feet behind second base and prepared to enjoy the game. Can you beat it? Well, the guards finally got the field cleared or at least got breathing room on it. They still crowded the outfielders and couldn't be budged past the foul lines, and as they soon sensed that the home plate was the center of action, they crowded around so close that the batters hardly had room to swing their bats. The wonder is that somebody wasn't killed.

As it was, an American soldier stopped a hot foul down the third base line with his jaw, an old Frenchman with a splendid white mustache, standing about six feet back of the catcher stopped a foul tip with his nose. You should have seen his moustache change from snow white to red. A wild peg from first to third hit a tiny little baby on the head and for a wonder didn't kill it. Add to all that the sight of two players carried off, one with a badly twisted ankle, and another badly spiked in the knee, and you would think they would have moved back. Not so. They didn't want to miss anything and they didn't.

It was a good game as I said and the base umpire pulled two bad decisions, so there was plenty of good old baseball yelling and honest, straight from the heart abusing of the umpire. Of course this game was mostly a mystery to them, but they got excited themselves when anybody made a hit, a run, or something with action to it. They couldn't understand why we thirsted for the umpire's heart or blood, or why the batter swung at the ball and missed it so often, or why a man should go to first without hitting the ball, or why on the third strike he should suddenly throw the bat down and run for first, or why the catcher invariably missed him when he threw the ball at him, and so on all around me I could hear them exclaiming "q'est ca se?" (what is that?) or "pourquoi, pourquoi" (why, why) and "Ooh, la la" which may mean anything from goodness alive to Oh, Hell.

I watched one Algerian who stood within ten feet of home plate all through the game, and I'll swear he wore a grin a yard long all afternoon. I thought he would split his face. One lady just back of us decided that we were all insane and said so to her neighbor. It was a circus to watch them. I don't know which I enjoyed more, the game or the crowd. I guess that's enough description, but believe me it was a day these people will never forget as long as they live.

This was Uncle Harold's last July 4 celebration. His last letter to his mother, dated January 26, 1919, made no mention that he was ill but he died just two weeks later. He had been overseas one and a half years and had so looked forward to getting back to his family and his fiancee. Grandma went to France after the war to accompany his body back to the United States. He is buried in the family plot in Augusta, along with his little sister, Fern, and other family members.

Dad, Gerald Chance, was born in 1898. He was a unique person who had a great influence on me. I will elaborate on his life in depth as I remember the many crazy stunts he pulled. Dad died in 1969 at age 70. Even his death and funeral were memorable events.

MOM & DAD — NEIGHBORHOOD FRIENDS

I find it hard to separate the lives of my mother and dad since they knew each other almost all their lives. Dad's family moved to Wichita from Augusta in 1905. At this time, the Chance family consisted of Martha and Mac Chance and their two sons, Harold (age 15), and Gerald (age seven). The Boggess family moved from Curtis, Oklahoma to Wichita about a year later, by coincidence settling in the same neighborhood as the Chances. They were Samuel and Helen and their seven children ranging in age from 19-year-old Ernest to one-year-old Florence. Lois, the sixth child, was about seven at this time. Both families lived in the first block of Ellis, about one mile east of the heart of downtown Wichita. Thus, Lois Boggess and Gerald Chance began their friendship.

Mom was a very pretty and happy girl. She played the cornet in the high school band, took ballet lessons, played on the girls' basketball team and loved outdoor activities with her family. They attended Kellogg grade school and Wichita High School, which was the only high school in Wichita at that time. Mom usually walked to Kellogg school while Dad rode his bike and kept an eye on her. Occasionally another boy would give her a ride on his bike or carry her books. This didn't sit well with Dad at all. He knew from an early age that she was the girl of his dreams.

Grandma dragged him to church a lot and I imagine he had a hard time sitting still for a full hour. School wasn't his favorite activity either. From an early age he loved adventure and this must have been difficult for his very conservative parents to understand.

Dad was very mechanical and was always building something involving transportation. He and his buddies from around the neighborhood went riding in the contraptions he built as he was growing up. When he was 17, he built a roller-coaster from the top of the barn at the back of their home to the street. Apparently it had a car or dolly that the boys rode down on for the thrill of their young lifetimes. I don't know how they got it back up; perhaps a pulley system or maybe they just pushed it back up. This, then, was the first "Chance ride."

They went canoeing, riding in his vehicles, bicycling, and camping in their teenage years. Dad worked with "Hammy" Hamilton, who owned a bicycle shop. Hammy built a bicycle built for 10 and Dad was one of the riders. He worked for Hammy in his teen years and entered at least one bicycle race that was pictured in the Wichita Eagle.

He dreamed up and built numerous machines. When he was 18 years old he built a car that had to be cranked. Once it kicked back (as they often did) and he broke his arm. We have many pictures of this broken arm, so he must have been quite proud of it. Many people considered him a mechanical genius, including Henry Ford, who somehow heard of Dad's ability and devotion to Ford products. Mr. Ford wanted Dad to come to work for him in Detroit, but Dad didn't want to leave Wichita. Also he treasured his freedom to go get a Coke with his friends in the daytime and then toil into the night to get his work done. He could never have held down a job with regular hours.

While Mom was a teenager her family regularly went camping at the Gordon bridge over the Walnut River in Butler County. They rode the train over there and spent the weekend. Dad often joined them, invited or not. The bridge was one of those nice old structures with a steel framework that looks as if it were made with an Erector set. A wide grassy bank nearby provided a place to camp and play.

As time passed this bridge came to mean a great deal to them, bringing back memories of those golden days. During Dad's last years, they drove over there at least once a week to see "their" bridge. Their grandson Jerry Ottaway took the nameplate off the old bridge just before authorities closed it and gave the sign to Dad for a Christmas present. This gift meant so much to Dad until his death a few months later.

MOM & DAD AFTER MARRIAGE

EARLY MARRIAGE AND LIFE IN THE CASTLE

I doubt that my folks ever had a formal date. They were just together in the neighborhood and in school. They did fall in love and both quit high school to get married when they were 18 and 19 years old. As the story was told to me, they decided to get married while his mother was in Kansas City for a church meeting. However, in a letter to his mother Uncle Harold said that it was awfully nice of Gerald to send her to K.C. to the meeting, that she needed to get away. In his next letter, after he found out that Gerald had gotten married, he said he could hardly believe it but he now understood why Gerald sent her to Kansas City. Gerald wasn't being nice, just sneaky so he could get married while his mother was out of town.

It was quite a shock to Dad's family. Grandma had just lost her husband in 1916, then Uncle Harold was sent to France in 1917, then Gerald had gotten married later that year. It meant she had lost everybody in a short length of time. Grandma and Harold didn't think they should have gotten married when they did or how they did.

But apparently the newlyweds were soon forgiven. Uncle Harold did not bawl Dad out but wished them happiness. Grandma let them stay at her house after they returned from living in Douglass, Kansas, for a short time, so discovered she had gained a daughter, not lost a son. There was never anything but good will between Mom and Grandma. Mother always said she had the best mother-in-law in the world. There was not a prouder uncle or grandma when Geraldine arrived 10 months after the folks were married.

My parents were married October 26, 1917 and the 26th has been a prominent date in our family ever since then. Geraldine was born on August 26, 1918, I was born December 26, 1919, and Harold, the last of the three children was born on September 25, 1921. He missed it by a day. My granddaughter Paula was born on December 26, 1969 (my 50th birthday) and Harold's daughter Nancy also was born December 26. So the folks had a daughter, a granddaughter, and a great-granddaughter all born the day after Christmas. Then Paula was married to Sam Holland, who was also born on that day. My daughter Betty was born April 26. Other grandchildren and great-grandchildren were born on the 26th of different months.

Not long after Mom and Dad were married, he got a job in a garage in Douglass, Kansas. This was about 25 miles from Wichita, but it might as well have been in Timbuktu as far as Mom was concerned. Douglass was a town of about 300 people at that time and there was nothing to do. Dad was working all day and she didn't know anybody else. She had been used to a big family and after all the excitement of getting married was over, reality was setting in. Soon they were back in Wichita and living in an apartment in Grandma Chance's house. Dad started his own garage near the house. This arrangement was good for Grandma and Mother as they were a lot of company for each other.

As soon as the folks could, they moved to a rental house about a mile from Grandma's and lived there for about five years. Sometime during that time, Mom packed up Geraldine, Harold and me to take a train trip to California. Grandma Boggess accompanied us out there and I think we were gone about two months. I was about three years old so don't remember much about it, except I slept in the upper berth with Grandma Boggess. I never heard much about that trip and just thought it was a fun vacation, but in later years, Geraldine said Mom was mad at Dad about something and went out there to visit Edna, Mom's oldest sister, to get away for a while. They seemed to work things out as I don't recall my parents ever having any trouble.

The family story about me was that I didn't want to swim in that dirty ocean. We have a picture of the seven of us cousins in a row with our sun umbrellas. As usual, I had one pant leg down and my hair was a mess. I couldn't be bothered with how I looked.

Then we moved to 1916 N. Wichita and lived there for about five years. Our house was three blocks from Waco Grade School. The school was a standard three-story red brick building but my kindergarten was in a wooden annex. I well remember the triangle the teacher would ring when it was time to go in from recess. Also that I turned cart wheels all the way to school and by the time I got there, my long curls were in tangles. Mom finally let me cut my hair.

The two first grade teachers were roommates. Miss Elbert was very tall and Miss McDaniel quite short, so they were an odd pair. Mr. Anderson was in charge of the school system's penmanship program and he would visit our class regularly to see how we were doing. We practiced the push-pull exercises and the series of circles until we got our coordination down. If we did well we were awarded penmanship certificates at the end of the year. Mr. Mayberry was superintendent of schools, a tall, distinguished man who often visited without notice. We were all very quiet when he entered the room.

I pretty well skipped second grade. With a December birthday, I had started school in January, so was a "mid-term" student in kindergarten and first grade. I was to have started second grade in January, then the following fall be moved up to third so I would be on track with the other students.

However, we Chance kids missed most of the second semester as we all got scarlet fever — one at a time — and none of us could go to school until we were all well. Mom about went crazy that year. We had a pink sign on our house saying we were quarantined. Dad could not live at home during our quarantine as he had to go to work, so he lived with Granny until we were well. However, I do remember him sneaking in and out of Mom's bedroom window many times.

When we were all well, we fumigated the house by burning some candles from the health department. Now, for scarlet fever, it is as simple as taking an antibiotic and hardly missing any school.

The third grade teacher was a rather short, plump lady named Miss Clymer who taught me my multiplication tables. She was quite an exuberant lady who threatened several times to jump out the window if we didn't know our lesson. As we were on the second floor, that usually got our attention.

There were a lot of children in the neighborhood. We had our little wagons and tricycles, flew kites, played running games, and always had a bunch of kids to play with. The father of one family was a street car conductor. He wore a black suit with a military-like hat with some brass on both as I recall. We lived at the end of the line and I remember him taking the trolley arm and swinging it from one end of the car to the other and moving his position to the other end. That was how the car changed directions. I can still hear the dinging of its bell.

I'm sure Dad wasn't setting the world on fire, but seemed to enjoy his work. He was working on Ford tractors in the fields at this time and knew more about Ford motors than almost anybody else. After working in the fields, he used to come home with bull snakes that he had found in the fields wrapped around his neck. He had the entire family squealing. As you will see as this unfolds, he was a great practical joker.

One of Dad's favorite tricks was to load us kids in the old Model T Ford, then wait for Mom to join us. She would come out to get in and he would drive off a way, then, just as she caught up, he would start out again. She would chase the car for a block sometimes and we kids thought it was hilarious. She seemed to go along with the gag.

Another day, she was helping us fly a kite in a vacant field when Dad came along and asked us to go with him. We all went with Dad and Mom was left holding the string. She looked rather silly out there flying the kite by herself. People would go by and ask her if she was having fun. I also remember Dad coming in with a bear suit on and walking on all fours. We were just sure that it was a real bear and pandemonium reigned. He did keep things lively around the house.

Mom spoiled Dad badly. He would point to something on the table that he wanted and she would pass it. Later my husband tried the same trick and was surprised that it didn't work with me.

It was when we lived on Wichita Street that I was called Sally Slowfoot. Apparently I was very slow either tying my shoes or putting them on. Dad started that name for me and it was then shortened to Sally. To this day, Harold calls me Sal. When I was born, Dad was hoping for a boy so they had no girl's name picked out. I suppose they planned to name the new baby Harold. After a day or two, the hospital needed a name for this poor little girl, so Mom told them to put down Leona. So that's how my birth certificate was made out. Well, Dad didn't like that name so renamed me Mary Elizabeth. I have two birth certificates plus the nickname of "Sal." Later on, I was often called "Chancie," especially in sports and when I lived in Denver. Ought to be enough names for anybody.

As we kids started needing less attention, Mom became active in Central Christian Church in the cradle roll department and the Missionary Society. She was always involved in PTA and with our teachers. After we were all in school, she would often treat herself to an afternoon at the movies but was always home by the time we got out of school.

When I was in fourth grade the school district changed the boundaries so we started to Irving Grade School. We had to walk by the big old mansions on Park Place and we had heard that they were haunted. We walked a little faster by those houses. The house of L.W. Clapp (the "father" of Wichita's fine park system) was just behind our little house. It was a mansion and they had the first electric car I had ever seen. I thought it was awesome and so quiet.

About six weeks after that school change, we had a chance to move to the Riverside area of Wichita. Argyle Forester, a friend of Dad's, owned the Forester (later Kirby) castle. He and his wife had moved out of the castle and neighborhood kids were throwing rocks through the beautiful stained glass windows. He wanted somebody to live in it so it would not be damaged any more.

I don't know what kind of discussion the folks had about moving in there, so I am not sure if they both wanted to move there or not. I know it was a big chore for Mom to keep up that huge place. I also know how much Dad enjoyed it. Anyway, in October of 1928, we moved to the castle at 1201 W. River Boulevard in Wichita. We transferred to Riverside school, just two blocks west of the castle.

As a side note, Mr. Forester was a wealthy Texan who owned a Cord automobile. It was a convertible and had a long hood area with chrome pipes coming down the sides of the hood. It must have been a very expensive car and I think only a few were made, and these only in the 1930s.

28

I have many memories of Riverside school. My fourth grade teacher, Miss Lowe, decided to try to change me to a right-hander. Mother set her foot down, though, so I did not have to go through that ordeal. I loved the giant strides, the turning bars, playing jacks on the sidewalk, the iron fire escape down the south side of the building, our May Fetes when we learned to wind the Maypole, playing softball on the south side of the building, and many of the people who went there.

The giant strides, in case you aren't old enough to remember, were iron handles hanging from chains from the top of a pole with two rungs to hold onto — one above the other. There were about eight of these mounted on a center pole. When they weren't in use, they hung at the pole. If you wanted to swing, you held onto the iron handles and started running to go around. When you went fast enough, you would leave the ground and swing your legs outward. When there were several of you on the strides, you could really go fast and fly high. One of the dangers was that the empty swings went around too and could hit you in the head if you were not careful. They were fun, but outlawed many years ago.

One day at recess, I was playing softball and my best friend, Betty Carpenter, was the catcher. When I swung the bat it flew out of my hand and hit Betty in the head. Although she wasn't injured seriously, I felt very bad about it. I spent a lot of time on the turning poles and learned to go around several times without stopping. One of the kids, Billy Glickman, was crippled by polio during that time. He was the first person I knew who had polio. There were many sets of twins in this school. They all had their pictures taken for the newspaper during that time. One year a child movie star went to Riverside for a while. He was a handsome boy and we were in awe of him.

I'm sure the era that the Chance family occupied the Forester Castle was the liveliest of all its years. We did not own a car while we lived there, but could walk almost anywhere we wanted to go and we had bicycles, motorcycles, and roller skates to get around with. Or we could ride with Grandma Chance, who bought her Model A Ford during that time. We could also ride with Grandma and Grandpa Boggess who lived only about three blocks away and had that center-door Model T that we rode to church in many times.

Since we lived just across the street from the Little Arkansas River, Dad started building boats in the basement of the castle. Several were made of mahogany and I remember all the time he spent sanding and resanding the wood to make the boats beautiful. He was always painstaking with all his restoration and building work and the quality certainly showed.

Some were race boats that he named after family members. The first one he named "My Squaw" after Mom, another the "Lois G" for my sister, Geraldine, and one for Harold called "Blue Eyes." My boat, called the "Mary E," was a launch. It had seats on either side of the hull and about three steps up to a prow that you could sit on. It had about a 25-horsepower motor (no doubt a Johnson) on the back and an awning that covered all the seating in the hull. I thought it was a beauty and was proud to have it named after me. The last I remember seeing the boat, it was stuck on a sand bar just north of the castle.

The basement of the castle was a very busy place with all the activity going on. A group of young men who lived in Riverside were quite interested in boats and racing, so they were always hanging around. Some of these were Dick and Will G. Price, Jr., Mark Benjamin, Sam Arnholz, and Leon Watkins. Dad also built a rifle range in the basement, complete with pulley ropes to bring the targets back without getting on the firing range. This is where we learned gun and rifle range safety from the best instructor we could have had, our Dad.

We also had to learn water safety before we could go out in boats by ourselves. The rule was that we had to swim across the river and back 25 times without stopping before we got our boats. It seemed like a long way back when I was a child, but now I look at that narrow river and wonder why I thought it was so far. We took to water like ducks and practically grew up in that river. Dad wouldn't let us go to the municipal pool as he said it was too dirty. He was probably right as far as germs were concerned. He believed running water, even though it was muddy, was healthier than a stagnant pool. We never minded that rule as we loved the river.

Dad never learned to swim, claiming that he couldn't as his body wasn't buoyant enough. It is amazing then that he had such a career in boat racing and stunts. Mom could almost go to sleep floating around in middle of the river, but she still kept one eye on us kids. She ordered us out of the water a few times when we didn't behave as we should. We didn't like to get out, though, so tried to obey her rules.

The Forester/Kirby castle, which had 27 rooms, was a wonderful old building that looked north across River Boulevard to the Arkansas River. The basement had an entrance through a cellar door on the south side. The Riverside gang usually went in that door while Dad was working. There were two stairways from the main floor, one for the servants and one for the residents. Of course, we had no servants, but when the castle was built, they were common. A dumb waiter went from the third floor to the kitchen, where everyone gathered.

The entry to the main floor through the back door was through what we called an "enclosure." This was an eight-foot-high stone wall and the area enclosed was probably about 20 feet wide and eight feet deep. We kept all the pop lids that we collected in this area. Nehi Bottling Company, a predecessor to Pepsi, had little corks in the lids and some were marked for winning prizes. We gathered them from wherever we could find them until we had time to see if we had won. I don't remember ever winning anything.

The kitchen was just inside the enclosure. A big bathroom was off to the left. The kitchen and bathroom floors were white hexagon-shaped tiles. With all the traffic in and out, it seemed Mother spent much of her time on her hands and knees scrubbing that tile floor. A library table in the middle of the kitchen served us for all sorts of things besides eating, including Ping-Pong. We had a carom board and many times shot so hard that the caroms would end up in the sink across the room. We also did our studying there.

Mom was well known for her angel food cakes. I always helped her and didn't see how she could ever make a cake without me. She would take her wire whip and beat the batter as I spooned in the flour and sugar. Dad was always getting the bright idea of having Mom make a cake late at night to go with the freezer of home-made ice cream he would make. She never seemed to mind and there were plenty of people around to help eat it.

A pantry with a built-in table where we ate some of our meals was just beyond the kitchen. Then beyond that was the dining room with rounded bay windows and a beautiful "grape" chandelier. It hung from the center of the room and the lights hung like bunches of green grapes. I don't remember having any furniture for this room and we never dined there.

The front entry hall faced the north and the river. The hall was a big open space with a large fish pond (which didn't work while we were there) built into the floor. A beautiful staircase with banisters led from the entry hall to the upper floors. The stained glass windows started at the first landing and went to the second floor. I don't remember the design in the glass but the date the castle was built, 1888, was part of it.

The living room, which we used often, had a fireplace on the south wall. Every room in the castle had a fireplace but they must have been gas-fired as I don't remember ever bringing in any wood. We had some furniture in this room, including a piano, and I remember sometimes gathering in there in the evenings as a family. One night I walked in my sleep down the front stairway and into the living room, practiced a couple of bars of music on the piano, then walked back upstairs. The family just watched me do it and didn't awaken me, but apparently had a hard time not laughing.

A room with a red sandstone fireplace to the ceiling was in one corner at the front of the house. The fireplace in that room was one we loved to climb and it seemed a long way to the ceiling, but it was only about nine or ten feet high I would guess. It had a lot of indentations to hang onto and we probably climbed it barefoot so we wouldn't damage it. The folks rented out this room to a lady who gave "expression" lessons. She gave us three kids free lessons in exchange for the rent. I thought that was fun and learned a lot of readings.

A sunken bathroom was just off the front hallway. Next to it, a bedroom, which we didn't use except at Halloween, connected back to the kitchen. In the middle of the castle, a winding, dark stairway used by the servants in the old days housed the dumb waiter. We seldom used this stairway, except to show it to our friends.

Now for the second floor, which you could get to by the beautiful staircase or the winding stairway. The folks had the bedroom just above the dining room with the rounded bay windows. Geraldine and I had the bedroom next to it. Harold's bedroom opened onto a screened-in porch on top of the portico. We used that porch a lot. Geraldine played with her dolls and we all played other games there.

Harold's room was not without adventures. One night lightning struck the house and the light cord that hung down over his bed. Fortunately, even though the cord and light were burned to a crisp, Harold was not hurt. Another night, our dog Peggy had 13 pups on his bed.

Other rooms on the second and third floors had been servants' quarters. We seldom went in that part. A large ballroom on the third floor had a false ceiling of stained-glass with over 300 light bulbs above it (so we were told). We went up there only for special parties or to visit a writer who rented a room next to the ballroom. I'm sure he didn't appreciate our visits as he was trying to write in peace and quiet. I guess we thought he was lonely up there.

The outside grounds were also very well used while we were there. The barn was on the south side of the grounds, which covered a full city block. Some man (I'm not sure who it was) built a biplane in the second story of the barn. He had to take the wings off when he tried to get it out.

A large croquet course and a dog pen for our Gordon setter, Peggy, and all her puppies were between the barn and the castle. Dad had lots of motorcycles that he worked on out in the barn, besides machines belonging to other people. One day a fire started in the barn while Dad was working on motorcycles. He put the fire out by smothering it with rags, but burned his hands in the process.

On the west, a long walkway covered by a trellis led to a gazebo, which was surrounded by catalpa trees. An asphalt driveway ran all the way around the castle and to the barn, then on to Harrison Street. I learned to ride a bicycle around this driveway. We had acquired one bicycle for the three of us and Harold made up the rules for learning. He said we got to ride until we fell off. So, he rode and rode and seldom fell off. Then I got a turn. I rode a few feet and fell off. Then it was his turn again. This went on for quite a while until I complained to Mom that I was never going to learn if I only got one fall. She gave me three falls and I finally learned. Then later we had an old motorcycle we could ride around on this road. One time I had to make a turn and didn't know how to stop, so ran it into the bushes.

(Of course, I am remembering a lot of this through the eyes of a child, which I find is not always accurate. When I went through the castle with my husband and daughters just before they tore it down, I found it had shrunk considerably.)

We lived there during the depths of the Great Depression and had very little money, as did most people. We spent 25 cents a day for food, had the use of the castle rent-free, probably paid a small utility fee, and lived in the lap of luxury. Most kids should have been that lucky. Our recreation consisted of free picture shows in the park, swimming in the river, boating in homemade boats, bicycling, crawdad fishing, rifle shooting on our own range, Girl Scouting, croquet, and playing Flinch, caroms, Ping-Pong or other games.

Our Halloween parties were memorable due to Dad's ingenuity. For a week one year we had all sorts of groups in for parties. The groups went through that unused bedroom next to the kitchen where we had put wet macaroni on the floor for them to squish through. Then we led them up the dark winding stairway to the second floor, where a siren went off and a casket with a dummy in it opened. If they weren't scared out of their wits by then, they went on up the same dark stairway to the ballroom on the third floor for the party. Dad was in his glory scaring so many people in one week.

Another Halloween, Geraldine announced we didn't need the folks to go with us in the neighborhood. So we went bravely out the door, only to notice two glowing eyes in the bushes just ahead. By this time Mom had locked the door on us. As we were screaming to get back into the house, Dad revealed himself from behind the bush with two burning cigarettes.

While living at the castle, we enjoyed fishing for crawdads. We got a nickel's worth of liver, tied bits of it on a string and caught crawdads in the river till our tub was full. Then we pulled the tub back to the gazebo, filled it with water and watched them squirm. Strange thing, they were all gone by the next morning. We always thought Mom and Dad took them back to the river, but now I'm sure they found their own way back.

Some neighborhood boys had hung a rope swing from a tree across the street. We had a lot of fun swinging on it, then dropping into the river. One day a boy named Eugene Brodie was swinging and fell in. Eugene couldn't swim so Harold, who was a third- or fourth-grader at the time, rescued him. This event made the local paper. I understand Eugene had to be rescued from drowning another time after that. Harold was named youngest boatsman in Wichita when he was eight years old and was written up in a third grade reader in Wichita.

The day we moved out of the castle, when the Kirbys bought it, was also memorable. The folks gave us a whole dollar for the three of us to get something to eat. We went to a little cafe near Porter and Briggs, climbed up on stools and ordered. I had finished my meal and was starting to eat my pie when we discovered $1.00 wasn't going to cover the pie. So I offered to give my pie back since I had eaten only one bite of it. They declined, however. This was the first time in our lives we had eaten in a restaurant and I was 11 years old.

I don't remember thinking we were special living in a castle. My folks were very unpretentious and just thankful for a place to live in those depression days.

THE BOATHOUSE AND RIVER FUN

It was the fall of 1930 when we moved out of the castle and a block down the street to 911 Faulkner. This was a brown, three-bedroom frame house, just a normal bungalow. We lived only two blocks from Grandma Boggess and were still about three blocks from Riverside School where I was in sixth grade. We were still close to the river, the parks, and the boathouse so it was no adjustment for us kids that I can remember.

I imagine Dad missed all the basement and garage space, but it was about this time that he opened his Indian Motorcycle shop at 806 N. Main. He did quit building boats but we were still doing a lot of boating. The city boathouse almost became our second home. Perhaps Dad kept his boats there. I'm sure Mom was glad to have a more manageable house than the castle and was happy to give up scrubbing the tile floors. (I have one of those tiles from when I went through the castle before it was torn down in the '60s.)

I remember "stunt night," my favorite time, during that period. About once a week Dad would get down on the floor and let us learn to turn backbends and flips over his back. We would also do rolls, cart wheels, and other stunts. We would have a race to see who could climb the door jamb first. We would do it spread-eagled in the doorway and inch our way to the top by moving one foot then the other. When we could reach the top, we jumped down.

I had my first experience with a stiff-hub bicycle on Faulkner. I loved to go up and down the block doing different stunts on a regular coaster-brake bike. I imagined all the people looking out their windows and enjoying the show I was putting on. Probably nobody was impressed but I had lots of fun riding backward, on the back fender, one-handed, no-handed, etc. Then one day I borrowed a neighbor boy's stiff-hub bicycle and while going full speed down the street stopped pedaling to rest. If you don't know, on a stiff-hub bicycle the pedals continue to go around while it is moving. I was not prepared for this and was thrown over the handle bars, landing on my head on the street. I got quite a bump and was rather embarrassed about this accident. I never again rode a stiff-hub.

The river and boathouse were important to all of us. We were down there nearly every day of the summer swimming, boating and having fun. Harold and I had our pictures taken in our white boating outfits and I am sure we thought we were pretty cute. We had on white bell-bottoms, white shirts, and a boating hat (like a captain's hat). We wore these outfits many times when we went out in our boats.

Mrs. Israel owned the boathouse and every evening she was out on the second-level balcony seeing that all went well. Canoeing being the "in" thing to do then, young lovers spent many a romantic evening on the river in rented canoes filled with pillows and wind-up Victrolas. Many people also rented rowboats for fishing or boating. A slow ride on a launch named the Julia Ann, which held about 20 people, cost 10 cents for a trip to the dam and back. Or they could take a speed-boat ride for 25 cents. In the evenings, it was lovely with music playing and lights shining on the water. Many years ago, the old boathouse was torn down to make way for an office building. Now the city has a new boathouse but that wonderful era will never return.

During the day, the river was filled with swimmers as well as all kinds of boats. Once I tried a kayak, a very tippy boat that's hard to paddle, and finally was able to go a way without dumping it over.

I can remember when I first got up enough nerve to jump off the 10-foot diving board into the river. I stood there for a long time before I finally made the big jump. Before long I started diving off the board. Then I was ready to jump off the lower level of the Murdock street bridge. Later I was diving off and then graduated to the top of the bridge railing. I thought I was pretty brave. Some people dived off the second story of the boathouse, but I was afraid I would hit the dock.

Besides, the river wasn't very deep there and we had to be careful to start coming up almost as soon as we hit the water. Once I tried a back flip off the dock and came back down on the dock instead of the water. I never tried that again.

Every year a big event at the boathouse attracted huge crowds. The banks of the river as well as the bridge and the boathouse were solid with spectators during this event. There were boat races on the river with Dad, Carl Evans, Dick and Will G. Price, Jr. and others racing for prizes. There must have been floats for a water parade also as we have a picture of Dad sitting on a raft with a car on it. Harold (Buddy) Siegel dived from the tower on top of the boathouse, a height of about 100 feet, many times. Sometimes at night he dived into a ring of fire that had been ignited on the river.

My Dad was billed in the paper as the daredevil of the river. As a warm-up and to tease the crowd, he would go to the third floor of the boathouse and stand there until he drew a crowd waiting for him to dive off, then he would back away. For one of his stunts, he did a daring ramp jump in his motorboat. He kept the crowd excited by making several passes in his boat before finally jumping, sometimes landing upside down. Because he could not swim he got back to shore by sinking to the bottom, then pushing up at an angle, sinking again and zigzagging through the water until he reached dry land.

We did a lot of surf-boarding in those days. Nobody was using skis then. Dad pulled a lot of surfers with his boat, including us kids. One day, a stranger asked Dad to pull him and he obliged. They got down to the bend of the river and this man fell off. He didn't come up, so Dad jumped out to save him. Dad couldn't swim, so he kept going down and coming up to the boat. He continued trying to rescue him but they concluded the man had died of a heart condition. Dad was terribly distressed about this and never again took a stranger for a ride.

Summertime recreation then was often outdoors and simple, good fun. We would take our blankets or sit on the hard wooden benches in South Riverside Park to watch silent movies. On Sunday nights we could go to a free band concert (in which Uncle Clifford played the horn) in the same park. Many nights we slept on the river bank when the temperature in our un-airconditioned homes became intolerable. We went to the bend of the river, but people were sleeping all up and down the river on the banks. In those days, we could walk to the park and home without fear of being attacked.

All of us Boggess cousins, along with our mothers and Grandma Boggess, enjoyed many a picnic in Sim Park. There seemed to be a sand hill that we all climbed and slid down (I do remember a few sandburrs on our seats and in our feet). We would get up baseball games, take nature hikes, and walk near the golf course. Occasionally we would spot a golf ball and pick it up, only to be yelled at by some irate golfer who strongly objected. After I took up golf, I understood their anger.

I belonged to a Girl Scout troop that met in the basement of Riverside Christian Church. We went on outings to Sim Park and Camp Bide-A-Wee. We learned to identify birds, trees and bushes and to appreciate nature. I remember working on a signaling badge. We learned to use flags to signal different letters, which I enjoyed a lot. I earned my first class badge during that time.

CENTRAL INTERMEDIATE AND THE PAPOOSE

We had now moved to 420 W. Ninth in Wichita where we lived for the next ten years. The three-bedroom frame house had the usual living room, dining room and kitchen, with one bathroom between the girls' room and Harold's bedroom. The folks had the front bedroom with French doors separating it from the living room. A single gas-burning pot belly stove in the dining room heated the whole house and we all tried to stand by it in the mornings until we got hot on one side then turned around to warm up on the other side.

The house had a large enclosed back porch and a detached garage. The big front porch had lovely spirea bushes in front of the railing. I always looked forward to the spirea blooming in the spring as that meant school was nearly out. And that in turn meant swimming at the boathouse, boating, surf boarding, and all the active, exciting things we did in the summer.

From early on, it was obvious that I was going to be involved in sports, games, and recreation. I can't remember when I didn't plan to be a physical education teacher. This was reinforced when I went to Central Intermediate School and had a gym teacher, Veola Enns, whom I adored. She encouraged me in this field and we remained life-long friends. Miss Enns had us line up for roll call by size. I was always next to the shortest girl but I became a leader and got a pin for having the most athletic points ever accumulated at this time. Gym was my favorite subject, I was out for intramurals every evening after school, and I participated in every game and activity offered.

Central Intermediate was about a mile from our home and we usually walked. We had all the short-cuts down pat. The old county courthouse was about half way and we went through the building in the

40

wintertime to get warmed up. Then we cut through the cathedral grounds and on to school. Sometimes after staying for after-school sports, I would walk downtown to the Kress dime store. We got 15 cents for lunch each day and spent only 13 cents, so at the end of the week I had a dime to spend. A bus ride was five cents but the Kress candy was very tempting. I had a choice: should I spend the money for a bus ride or walk home with a sack of candy? I usually chose to buy the candy.

Geraldine had warned me about how tough it was in intermediate school. She came home from school in her first semester as a 7B all upset. She said no matter what she did, she was going to get a conference. If she ran to get to her next class she would get in trouble and if she didn't run, she would be late for class and get a conference. However within a few days she discovered she could get there on time without running. The 8th and 9th graders initiated the newcomers with a ditty that went:

Climb upon my knee, 7B.
There's no way of knowing,
There's no way of showing,
What you mean to me, 7B.

Most of the kids in my home room came from Riverside grade school, so they were all my friends. Our teacher was Miss Hall and she was a bit cross-eyed, but a very nice teacher. This home room had all the brains of the school in it and most of them took Latin, Miss Hall's subject. I don't know why they put me there. I made above-average grades but my interests were elsewhere; especially sports, including basketball.

Girls' basketball went through a lot of changes in the years I was involved in it. At Central we all had to stand in circles and pass the ball from circle to circle to get it into the basket. At North High School we played half-court, meaning the guards could not shoot, but were to get the ball and pass it to the forwards on the other end of the court. A few years later, they allowed one guard from each side to be a rover and she could go the entire length of the court. They called this the "roving guard" version. As I started teaching in the '60s, they made the girls' rules the same as boys' and it remains that way today.

◁◁◁◁ ▷▷▷▷

Dad's Indian Motorcycle shop on North Main was only about five blocks away from our home. There was quite a group of young men who hung around the shop. When they weren't there, they were at our house or at the boat house. We called them the motorcycle gang, but that term didn't have the same connotation as it does today. These were just people who loved to ride cycles, go to or participate in races and take Sunday afternoon rides. They were clean-cut fellows who got together for motorcycle shoptalk, much as pilots do when they "hangar fly."

Frank Chacon, who was a professional starter for races, an excellent mechanic, and a good rider, went to work for Dad. They secretly decided to build us kids a little motorcycle for Christmas. They cut down a twin-cylinder motorcycle, made the frame to fit it, ordered small-size tires, and made a sidecar to go with it. The gas tank held one gallon and the cycle could probably go 50 or so miles on one tank of gas, which was five cents a gallon at that time. They called it the Indian Papoose and it was the only one ever built.

We kids were banned from the shop for six weeks before Christmas and Dad had us guessing what they were giving us. I thought it might be a swing set. Geraldine thought a doll house. Harold never did say what he thought it might be, but never guessed a motorcycle.

On Christmas morning, all the gang was there. We kids were taken to the shop and told to start looking. Harold spotted a regular motorcycle and picked that. Dad told him to keep looking. He came upon this little red jewel with his name on it and was ready to take off on his own. He was only 10, but had no doubt he could ride it. Meantime, Geraldine and I had found the little red sidecar with our names on it. Dad attached the sidecar to the cycle then let Harold drive it through the alley. Then it was time for photos. They had hired a professional photographer so we have lots of pictures of that day. The paper ran our picture at that time, then again when the motorcycle was 25 and then 50 years old.

The day after Christmas I turned 12 years old and had a birthday party, my first, with several of my girl friends. I took Betty Carpenter, the one I hit in the head with the bat, for a ride in the Papoose. Somehow I didn't quite make a little hill and ran the sidecar, with Betty in it, into the garage. It just spoiled my party and the sidecar had to get a repair job already. Dad then laid down the new rules: first we had to sweep out the alley behind the house so we wouldn't puncture the tires, then we could drive the Papoose only in that alley for three months before he would allow us to go up and down Ninth Street for three blocks. After another three months, we were turned loose, but still with restrictions.

We always said Dad had spies all over town. If we didn't stop dead still at a stop sign, we would be grounded. The worst thing we ever did was to go on a little excursion without telling the folks where we were going. We always blamed Geraldine for this. She had gotten a map and decided Goddard, a small town about 10 miles west of Wichita, would be just a short trip. After all, it was only about an inch on the map. So we took out and were west of Wichita somewhere when we ran out of oil and burned up the engine. Dad had everybody out looking for us, but never dreamed we would be so far from home. For our punishment he did not fix the engine for a very long time.

After Dad fixed the engine, Harold had a Liberty magazine route and we all delivered magazines in the cycle. In fact, the magazine put our picture in one of their editions. We also drove the Papoose to school, even though the principal was very much against it. Licenses weren't required then, so we were doing nothing illegal but he still didn't like the idea. Geraldine thought she was too sophisticated to ride all the way to school, so she would get off about a block away. Harold and I, though, rode all the way. The Papoose became quite a famous little motorcycle during this time and we always had lots of friends to occupy the sidecar.

Just a word about Dad's shop. It was always cluttered but Dad knew where every tool was. He had only one place for visitors to sit in the back of the shop. That was an old black car seat that was on the floor. It was very inviting, but little did they know that Dad had electrified that comfortable-looking chair. He would wait till somebody was comfortable and unsuspecting, then turn on the juice. The victims would come flying out of that chair like a shot. This happened time after time and everyone thought it was hilarious. One day an older man came in and made himself comfortable and Dad gave it a shot. The man leaped out of the chair quite stunned and Dad was afraid he had hurt himself or had had a heart attack so gave it up after that.

Later Dad moved his shop one block south to the 700 block of North Main, present location of Red Cross building. It was on the west side of the street between two poultry stores. I don't remember a bad smell, but, between the poultry and the grease in his shop, it must have been pretty fragrant.

One Halloween night he put Harold and his friend Othall "Oats" Huntsinger, who were about 13 or 14 at this time, up to a trick. Spec Tapp was a motorcycle policeman and a great one to pull jokes on others but he couldn't take a joke on himself. Spec had a habit of coming in to the shop and leaving his cycle out back with the radio on and had done so this Halloween. When Spec came in to chat with Dad, the boys walked the cycle about eight blocks south down Main street to City Hall. When Spec went outside a little later and found his motorcycle missing, he was furious. He started walking south on Main and met the boys walking back after parking it at City Hall. Needless to say, he was madder than hops and threatened to have the boys arrested. I'm sure he took a lot of razzing from his fellow officers. Maybe Dad went too far with this trick.

I don't know how the neighbors put up with the Chance family as our place was always a beehive of activity. Motorcyclists met there on Sunday afternoons for a drive. Dad kept raccoons, skunks, and other animals in cages in the back yard. We made a baseball field out of our back yard. There was a basketball goal attached to the garage and we had a lot of pick-up games of basketball. We roller skated on the sidewalk and played hockey in the street with tin cans and sticks. We played New York and Boston (early charades), run-sheep-run, and Annie-over, among other outdoor games. We tied strings of tin cans to cars as they approached a nearby stop sign, then gleefully waited for the cars to start up, making a terrible racket. The drivers would get out and take off the string of cans, then we would come out of hiding and do it again to the next car.

If any of our neighbors complained, I don't remember it. Actually, all the neighborhood kids hung around our house, so maybe the noise was a fair trade. Fortunately, we also spent a lot of time at the boathouse and swimming in the river.

Another exciting thing we did was go on our first airplane ride. Dad took us out to the farm of a friend who had been tinkering with planes for some time. This man had built a plane out in his barn, tried to fly it and crashed. He rebuilt the plane, tried again and crashed again. He kept building and crashing until, after his 13th try, he finally managed a successful flight. His name was Clyde Cessna and he went on to become one of aviation's great pioneers and founder of the Cessna Aircraft Company.

Mom always took us to Sunday school and church at Central Christian in Wichita, where we had excellent teachers. I still remember how we learned the books of the Bible that Mrs. Elgin and Mrs. Kinder taught us. We also learned the disciples' names through songs.

Our minister at that time was Dr. Frank Lowe, a young bachelor and an enthusiastic preacher, who started the Temple Star program. You had to be 12 to join as that was the age at which Jesus went into the Temple. We had a six-pointed star pin with a picture of Jesus in the center. We won awards for learning passages and had an awards dinner once a year at the YWCA. What I remember most was the delicious strawberry pie with a lattice crust and whipped cream on top.

The junior high years were very enjoyable for me. I learned a lot about different sports and games, drove the motorcycle with my friends as passengers, drove and rode in all sorts of boats, and was still on my way to being a physical education teacher. My parents, especially my Dad, encouraged me all the way.

COLORADO CARNIVAL

In 1934 our family went on the road with some little race cars that Dad had built. He also built the trailer they were carried on. We went to several towns east of Wichita, such as Madison and Eureka. We would find a vacant lot, scrape it smooth for a track, and be in business for about a week. Then we headed west toward Kinsley, Larned, and Dodge City before going on to Manitou, Colorado. We went there because it had been a lot of work to set up a new track every week and motels weren't too plush in those days and because Manitou was a popular tourist spot.

I was 14 years old then and Dad had taught me to drive a car. Mother didn't drive after Model T days and Harold was too young. We were between Lamar and Las Animas, Colorado, when Dad got sleepy and asked me to drive. But I guess he didn't trust me too much as he was only half asleep in the back seat. Every time I went over a bridge, he said, "Woop, woop, woop!" We always said he "wooped" me over every bridge in eastern Colorado. I remember seeing the shadows of the clouds and how fascinating it was to go in and out of the shadows. Guess I had never been in such wide open spaces before.

As we approached the mountains, I was enamored by their vast size and their beauty. Having been raised on the flatlands of Kansas, I could not believe their immensity. The folks told me the mountains were a lot farther away than they looked. It seemed we drove for miles and still were not near them. That view of Pikes Peak as you go west from Colorado Springs toward Manitou is still one of my favorite scenes. I remember sitting by the hour at our cabin in Manitou just looking at those beautiful hills.

46

Those hills almost took our lives that year, however. Grandma and Grandpa Boggess had come out in their 1929 Dodge to visit us. We also had a Dodge about the same vintage and took the two cars up to Green Mountain Falls for a picnic on a beautiful Sunday afternoon.

On our way back, the Boggesses, Dad and Harold were in the front car with Grandpa driving. Herb Ottaway, who was dating my sister and owned the little steam train that was part of our carnival, was driving our car with Geraldine, Mom and me as passengers. Coming down along Ute Pass, the road was terribly twisted, with a high rocky mountain on our left and a deep ravine on our right.

Suddenly Herb yelled that he had no brakes and no gears. Our left rear wheel had come loose and we had lost our hydraulic fluid. We kept going faster and faster and Herb asked, "What should I do now?" Mom, in all her mechanical wisdom, blurted out, "Honk the horn!"

When he did, Dad turned around to see what our trouble was and saw a wild gleam in Herb's eyes. With that, he told Grandpa to speed up so our car could hit theirs at about the same speed. When we hit the back of their car, our wheel came flying off and I can still see it rolling into the mountain. We hit them again, then both cars ground to a stop. We were going about 60 miles an hour down that mountain when we hit.

Had we not done that, it would have been either hit the mountain or go into the ravine. When we got stopped, Mom got out and sat on the running board and promptly passed out. Of course, she said she was only taking a rest. Our first trip into the mountains almost became our last.

That summer, the first of several spent in Colorado, we set up our track on the east edge of Stonewall Park, a cabin camp between Colorado City and Manitou on the road to Garden of the Gods. It was just a group of very rough log cabins surrounded by a stone wall, hence the name.

The park was operated by a man named Earl and his son, Doc, who was slightly retarded. They came from Oklahoma every summer to run this operation. Earl was a Pikes Peak tour car driver who knew this area like the back of his hand. He pointed out many of the rock formations in the Garden of the Gods that I can still find and identify.

Also, he took us on our first trip up Pikes Peak. The cost for riding in his open-air Pierce Arrow was $5 each. Mom had said the first day we took in $50 we could go up the Peak. We charged 10 cents for our rides, so $50 meant we had to have a lot of customers. Toward the last of the season, we finally accomplished this goal. Our first trip up there was quite a thrill. It was very cold at 14,101 feet and I got a headache from the altitude but the view was worth it.

The four small race cars, all painted different colors, had little platforms on the back where we could ride until we thought the kids were ready to drive by themselves. Occasionally we would have to hop back on if they got out of control, but mostly we could just holler at them to straighten them out. The throttle and the brake were both hand-controlled.

Harold and I taught a lot of kids to drive the cars, which would go only 15 miles an hour at top speed. We would set the throttle lower for the little ones, many of whom were only three years old, so it was not dangerous for them. I think the worst injury any kid ever had was a bumped nose when one would hit the fence or another car. The look on their faces when they got off was one of great joy and achievement.

Along with the cars, we had Herb Ottaway's little steam train and also the Papoose to give rides in. The Papoose was painted white that year, but soon went back to the original red color.

The Osage Indians in Oklahoma had just been awarded their oil rights money from the government and they arrived in Manitou by the droves. Most drove big fancy cars and were drinking heavily. They would send their kids over to the track to ride all evening while they caroused. Some kids would have $10 worth of tickets and when we told them "one more lap," they would just throw out another ticket and never get out of the car. I remember one cute little Indian boy named Bubbie who was about four years old. He never smiled, as none of them did, but he loved to drive those cars. He was our favorite and I often wonder what became of him.

An Indian lady from Perry, Oklahoma, asked Dad to build three race cars for her, so he figured she had three kids. He built them and we delivered them to her home that winter, only to find out she had no children. She just had three of everything and wanted three race cars for the neighbor kids to drive.

One time I played the part of Carry Nation, the prohibitionist from Kansas. An Indian man, who was obviously inebriated, wanted to ride the cars and he asked me to hold his whiskey bottle. I was 14 years old and was insulted that he would ask me to do that. I took his bottle and while he was riding, I poured the liquor out. When Mom found out I did that, she really reprimanded me. Mostly she was afraid of what the Indian might do when he found his bottle empty. However, nothing happened.

We stayed at the Stonewall cabins for a couple of weeks, then moved in with the Matsons, a family from Kansas Dad knew who were probably trying to make an extra dime off the tourists. All of us plus Herb Ottaway stayed with them a month or so. We became acquainted with several families we did business with. The Hershey family ran a drive-up restaurant. We went there many times after we closed for the evening. Patsy's Popcorn and Salt Water Taffy store in Manitou was also a favorite of ours and we got to know the owners quite well.

A couple named Lister owned an open-air market just east of Stonewall. They had a peanut machine there and Dad was always putting his penny in and getting a handful of nuts. One day, he didn't think he got his money's worth and stuck his hand up to get more. His hand got jammed and they had to take the machine apart to free him. Finally, a joke on Dad.

Manitou had one police car and policeman, which seemed to be ample at the time. We would wave at him when he went by on patrol. He stopped by to chat with us once in a while, but we never had reason to call the police at our business. The season started about July 4 and closed on Labor Day. We would pack up our trailers on Labor Day evening, after the Pikes Peak Races were over, as Manitou was like a ghost town on the next day. Those were the days when school started the day after Labor Day, so the town was deserted and all businesses closed.

At the end of the season, it became our custom to take a short vacation in Colorado before returning home. We probably missed a day or two of school but made it up later. In 1934 we headed for Denver to visit Uncle Bob, Mom's brother. He lived near Sheridan on West Colfax Avenue, which was in the country then. I went out in the back yard and saw this cow coming my way and didn't realize there was a fence between me and the cow. I started running and fell on a very sharp rock and tore a hole in my knee. They took me to a doctor and he clamped my knee shut. It seemed to take forever for it to heal and left a scar that still shows. Probably I kept doing things that broke it open again. Anyway, I was so disappointed as I had been looking forward to swimming class at North High. As it turned out, I couldn't swim until second semester.

Thus I started my career at North High in Wichita. This is still the most beautiful high school in this part of the country. It is a sandy-colored art deco building with an Indian motif. Indian heads, arrows, and Indian designs are used throughout the building, so of course we were known as the North High Redskins. The Arkansas River, which flows just to the west, made a perfect place for our Water Carnival in May. The Minisa Bridge next to the school uses the same designs as the building. The school was built in 1929, so it was fairly new when I was there and, as usual, the gym was my favorite area.

NORTH HIGH SCHOOL

By now Dad was working for Arnholz Coffee Company and was in charge of the trucks that went all over Kansas during the week delivering coffee to restaurants. He had to service them over the weekend, make any repairs, and have them ready to go by the first of the week. All these trucks had the Arnholz rooster painted on the sides and most of them were painted by Sam Lewellen or "Smitty the Jumper," both of whom were excellent sign painters. Smitty became famous around the Midwest for his parachute jumping, making his last jumps tandem when he was well into his nineties. He was rather eccentric, liked to hug the ladies and was his own best PR person. He had his personal car painted all over with "Smitty the Jumper" signs, so you had no doubt who he was.

Since most of Dad's work was done on the weekend, he restored old cars during the week. The first one I remember was Sam Arnholz's 1911 Maxwell. The engine had lots of nickel plating and it was beautifully restored, winning many prizes at antique car shows. Dad also worked on Jack Hinkle's cars and some of his own. Hinkle was a car racer himself and sponsored Indianapolis 500 driver Jack McGrath, who finished fifth in 1953 and third in 1954. Dad was in the pits in Gasoline Alley both those years at the Indy.

He was also the first president of the Horseless Carriage Club in Wichita. He and Mom dressed in proper attire for all their outings. Mom looked so pretty in her old long dress.

Dad and Bob Arnholz, Sam's dad, became the best of friends. Bob had a cabin on a small lake near Cheney where we were always welcome to spend a weekend or take our Sunday School classes. Bob and Dad were both great outdoorsmen so they hunted and fished together a lot. Dad built a riding lawnmower for Bob to use at the lake. Then he thought the company needed a coffee-sacking machine. So he invented one and kept it working. That was the first mechanization for the company.

What with going out for sodas with friends, Dad didn't get too much work done in the daytime, but he worked through the night to get the trucks ready. We kids were there with Mom a lot keeping Dad company in the evenings. I can remember how good the shop smelled when all the trucks came in for the weekend with that delicious coffee aroma. Even though Dad and Mom didn't drink coffee, Dad would argue with anybody till the cows came in that Arnholz coffee was the best coffee ever brewed. He was a very loyal employee and was with them nearly 20 years.

Just a word about Mom during these days. She was always home when we got out of school and saw that we got to Sunday School and church every Sunday. She always had a meal ready when Dad got home, no matter what the time or how many friends he brought with him. Mom was active in the church, but it didn't get in the way of her family. She walked nearly everywhere she went but was always ready for a motorcycle ride, a spin in an old car or anything else that came along. She seemed to enjoy life, no matter what it brought.

We still lived near Ninth and Waco so we always walked to and from North High, which was only about four blocks away. We had only 10 cents to spend on school lunches at North. We always got up before the folks did and made our own breakfast. Before going to school, I would get a dime out of Dad's pants pocket and usually felt bad about it as I knew he didn't have much money. However, things were looking up for us, with Dad having a full-time job and our carnival showing promise.

In the fall of 1934 I felt pretty grown-up going to high school. There were several of us girls who teamed up together and were undefeated in intramurals in all sports for all three years. We played softball, basketball, and soccer. We were also involved with swimming, rifle, and individual sports such as Ping-Pong, horseshoes, badminton, and tennis. I earned many rifle medals and the equivalent of a letter with points accumulated in all sports. I remember sitting in my sixth-hour class anxiously waiting for school to dismiss so I could go back to the gym for after-school sports.

Remember that this was during the Dust Bowl days and we endured our share of them at North. The school authorities did everything they could to keep the dust from coming into the school. They covered the windows as best they could with rags, but I can remember the grit on our papers as we tried to write. Even when the wind wasn't blowing, the silt crept in. Some students and teachers put damp rags over their mouths and noses so they could breathe.

It was tough walking home in that dust. When we got home, things were just as bad, as our homes were not built as tightly as they are today. Much of the silt was the red soil from Oklahoma. Those were not pretty days in Kansas. The authorities did plant lots of trees and taught farmers how to plow their fields to prevent that from happening again. Apparently it worked as we haven't had that kind of disaster since.

We had study hall in the school cafeteria. There were two very stern teachers tending study hall who allowed practically no nonsense. I was a proctor in the halls during my senior year with a post on third floor facing the river and the Minisa bridge. I remember looking out the window when there were no students in the halls and dreaming of being outdoors, looking forward to going to Colorado, and anything but being in school. I should have been studying.

I was not one of the intellectual students, but got above-average grades. I participated in Pep Club, Girl Reserves, and other special activities. For Impersonation Day one year, some buddies formed a hillbilly band and I played the harmonica. We had dress-up day for May Day activities another year and I wore a hobo outfit.

One of the special events put on by the women physical education teachers one year was the "Pow Wow." The gym was decorated with "The Good Ship Lollipop" at one end and other decorations on the walls. The gym classes (with white shorts and shirts) put on quite a show with marching drills, tap dancers, tumblers, gymnastic exhibits, fan-shaped pyramids with groups of five girls making up the design, and a finale of beautiful ladies doing the waltz. All this was in costume and was really an extravaganza. I was in several of the events.

Another special event, Field Day, was an all-day event at Linwood Park in conjunction with East High. It was a competition between classes rather than schools so there was none of the North/East rivalry. This was a day of softball, cage ball, all sorts of races, a greased-pole climb, food and soft drinks. Even the teachers participated in this event with their own softball game. We were all tired and dirty by the end of the day, but the class winner was declared before all went home. It was good clean fun and competition in our day but had to be discontinued later as a few students got out of hand and spoiled it for the majority.

The rivalry between North and East, the only two high schools in Wichita at the time, was fierce. We were the Redskins and they were the Aces. We had our river, they had a canal. We were always proud of our Water Carnival held in May of each year, weather permitting. This event began with canoe and swimming races, followed by a parade of beautifully-decorated canoes. We dared East to have a water carnival in their canal.

My good friend Betty Carpenter wrote in "The Tower," the North High annual: "May there always be a spirit of rivalry predominating between my Redskins and their brother Aces. The greatest days of the year will be when these two meet in friendly conflicts, and when they fight together on the celebrated 'Field Day.' As night fell the spirit could see that his school was no longer an inanimate construction. As he beheld it, he saw that it was good. May the Redskins who will live in my building add to as well as keep the ideals which are now a part of the school."

The North/East rivalry grew less intense as more high schools were built in Wichita but even today when I meet somebody who graduated from East, I give them my sympathy. It was all in good fun. As we all merged into Wichita University, we forgot what schools we came from and became loyal to the University.

I remember getting my first pair of nylon hose for graduation. Most girls would have been ecstatic, but I was mad at my Aunt Bess for getting me something that I never intended to wear. Bess Arnold was my Grandma Chance's sister and she thought it was time I became more lady-like. I didn't even want to go to my graduation because I hated dressing up. We did not have caps and gowns for graduation back then in 1937. I can't remember if I wore the hose, but I did go to the ceremony — probably under protest.

Those were lean times for all, but we were looking forward to the next step. For some it was marriage, for others jobs, and college for others. The war was not looming yet and we were all better off than when we started high school. Our family had gone to Colorado with our carnival every summer, so there was enough money for me to go to Wichita University. I was eager to continue my education toward my goal of becoming a physical education teacher. The tuition was $50 per semester, plus books and supplies. Sounds pretty cheap now, but so were the wages at the time.

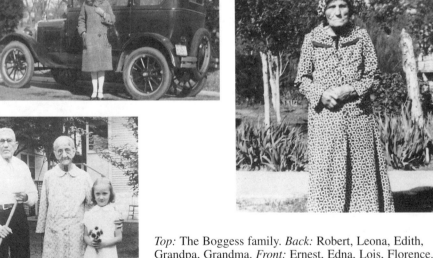

Top: The Boggess family. *Back:* Robert, Leona, Edith, Grandpa, Grandma. *Front:* Ernest, Edna, Lois, Florence.

Upper left: Leona with the family's 1927 Model T.

Above: Great-grandma Walstad in 1937 at age 89.

Left: Great-grandpa and Grandma Chance in 1940 with their great-granddaughter Rita Long. Photo taken one week before Grandpa died at age 96.

Above: Enjoying the Walnut River near the Gordon Bridge, 1915.

Left: Lois and Gerald in the car he built, 1917.

Below: Martha D. (Granny) Chance in 1960 with her 1929 Model A.

Lois and Gerald shortly after their wedding, with their dog Goldie in 1917.

Gerald's first shop, 1918. (He must have cleaned it up before taking the picture.)

Left: Mary, Harold and Geraldine Chance at ages four, two and five.

Below: East side of Forester-Kirby castle where we lived in the 1930s. *PHOTO BY PHILIP DIFILIPPO*

Bottom: Southeast side of the castle. *PHOTO BY PHILIP DIFILIPPO*

Motorcycle "gang" ready for a Sunday ride. Left to right: first two unidentified, Ina and
Frank Chacon, Mom and Dad, we three kids on Papoose, Pauline and Leroy Stimpson.

Riverside Boathouse and Murdock Bridge during the river festival, 1929. Dad is on the front
of the raft and Carl Evans, Plymouth dealer, is at the back.

Indian "Papoose" Dad made and gave to us for Christmas, 1931. Geraldine and Harold are behind me, Dad to the right.

We three, Dad and the Papoose 25 years later, in 1956.

Left: The three Chance "kids" in 1981 with the Papoose, then 50 years old and restored.

Below: Four race cars Dad built, with the Papoose at the track in Manitou, Colorado, 1937.

Bottom: The Ottaway steam train, 1937.

Above left: The 1929 Dodge that took us on a wild ride down Ute Pass in 1934. Here Harold, Mom, our dog Peggy and I are on the road to Pikes Peak in '37.

Above right: In costume for North High Impersonation Day, 1937.

Right: Practicing my swing during high school days.

Below: North High "Pow Wow" with Good Ship Lollipop theme and human fans. I'm on the left end of the first fan on right.

COLORADO AND
EARLY YEARS AT WICHITA UNIVERSITY

One of the gifts I received for graduation from high school was a five-year diary. I was faithful in keeping a short record for each day of that period, beginning in June, 1937. I started a second diary and kept it until March of 1944. This probably accounts for many of the details recounted in this book. How I wish I had kept it up longer.

Right after graduation from high school, a group of us gals formed an Old Maids Club. We got together regularly to gab or eat or just have fun. The first one to end her bachelorship was married shortly after graduation. Her sister married about four years later. Another of our number wasn't far behind, then still another married a year or so later. Then there was a long gap until I joined the crowd in marriage in 1947. The last was married in 1949. However, we didn't let a little thing like marriage spoil our club. As time went on, we got together with our husbands and children many times. We have scattered to different parts of the country, but when any of them come to Wichita, we always have a get-together of any who are around. The oldest celebrated her 75th birthday in 1994 and I got up and told about the Old Maids. Everybody there had heard of us. One Old Maid died several years ago, but the rest of us are hanging in there.

In June of 1937 Dad bought the first new car we ever had, a light green four-door Ford sedan. We all went down to the Ford dealership to pick it out and I can still remember the new smell of that car. We drove it to Colorado shortly after we bought it.

By now we had moved our carnival location to Manitou Avenue, about one mile east of downtown Manitou. We also moved into tents.

Dad built wooden floors, but it was a daily chore to sweep out the sand. Geraldine had married Herb Ottaway in 1935 and they had been bringing their Ottaway train out. They had their tent and we had ours nearby. We stayed at this location and lived in tents every summer through 1941.

The CCC (Civilian Conservation Corps) was building a new road just north of Manitou. It was called the Rampart Range Road and would be a scenic road to Woodland Park, about 20 miles up Ute Pass. For some unknown reason, we decided to try it out, even though it was still under construction. Dad had gone back to Wichita on July 5, and so I assume that Harold was driving on this excursion on July 8. My notation in my diary was that we had to be pushed up a hill and the car was damaged in the process. We turned around when we came to the end of the finished road so it was a stupid trip. I made several changes in my diary, probably so Dad wouldn't find out about our little accident with the new car.

We hired a friend of Harold's, Whitey Williams, to work for us for several summers and his dad also worked as an engineer for the little train. By now, Mom had her hands full keeping us on the job. There were so many exciting things to do, such as horseback riding, going up Pikes Peak and other places in the area. We were getting to be well known in the area now as this was our fourth summer. Lots of friends and relatives came to visit so we became good tour guides.

Harold kept the equipment running, Herb took care of the train, Mom was the boss and chief ticket seller. Geraldine also sold tickets. I was chief flunky and was conned into working when Harold had something better to do. I could drive all the rides, sell tickets, and do about everything except the mechanical work. I recorded the amount we made every day, as well as Herb's income on the train. It didn't seem like much sometimes, but our expenses weren't very high either.

Every September when Dad came out to pack us up and take us home, we would take a special trip. This year after closing in Manitou we went to Denver to visit Uncle Bob, the Museum of Natural History, and the Denver Zoo. Then we drove back to Manitou and took another side trip to the Royal Gorge through Phantom Canyon, on to

Victor and Cripple Creek mining towns, and back to Manitou. On the third day, we drove to Buena Vista, Leadville, Twin Lakes, and Aspen, then stayed at Glenwood Springs that night.

Dad liked to look in all the junk stores, which bored me, but I have several valuable items from these trips. One is an old clock that mimics a fountain with a lion's head. Instead of a stream of water coming out of the lion's mouth, the "stream" is a twisted glass tube that looks like water when it rotates. I also have the beautiful Regina music box that now adorns my living room. It has a large box made of cherry wood that stands on carved legs. On lifting the lid you find a metal disc about 15 inches in diameter punched with holes. When the spring is wound up, the disc rotates like a phonograph record and metal fingers pluck the holes, much as a player piano operates. The tones are beautiful, deep and resonant. A drawer holds extra discs. It's a real treasure.

From Glenwood Springs, we went to Rifle and Craig Colorado. By mistake, we went the wrong direction and ended up in Wyoming. It was a long, desolate drive, with no food and no restaurants along the way. Finally made it to Steamboat Springs, Granby, Grand Lake, Estes Park and Boulder. We really saw a lot of Colorado on that trip — and a little of Wyoming.

Our trip back to Kansas was in the rain all the way and we were in flood waters several times. At Kingman, Herb and Geraldine got across a bridge, but it washed out before we could get across. We spent the night in the car waiting for the water to go down and to find another way across the water.

Two days later I started at Wichita University where I was soon involved in intramural sports. Field hockey and badminton were the fall sports. I did all right in my classes, except physiology. I had made A's in high school, but the doctor teaching this class was a very tough teacher. I ended up flunking this class, along with over half the students. I spent the rest of my college career making up for those minus credits.

Wichita University had an ROTC unit, which sponsored rifle teams. In early 1938, I started practicing for the team. Our first practice range was in the fourth floor attic of the science hall, right next to

58

the wind tunnel. When the wind tunnel was turned on, it was so loud we couldn't even hear our rifle shots. We used Army 22 rifles and had ROTC instructors. I had been shooting since I lived in the castle and had earned many medals from the National Rifle Association in high school, so was ready to learn all I could at Wichita University.

The girls' team went to Kemper Military Academy in Booneville, Missouri, every spring for the national collegiate rifle contests and had a winning record. In order to make the team, anybody who came out for rifle shot 10 targets to qualify for Kemper. The five girls with the top scores got to make the trip. In my freshman year, I missed the top five by 1/10th of a point and was first alternate. Nobody got sick, so I didn't go in 1938. In February of 1938, I shot my first 100 (called a possible) target. On March 20, I won the Women's State Rifle Championship, which was not a school-sponsored event.

In the spring of 1938, I began to do a lot of baby-sitting for Marc and Dorothy Benjamin. It seems I practically raised Benny, their son, for a couple of years. I was getting the grand sum of 35 cents an evening, or 50 cents if I stayed after midnight. For this, I was expected to fix his supper, do the dishes, and care for him. Benny must have been a good kid, as I don't remember that I minded taking care of him, and I appreciated the money as I was saving to buy a new rifle.

I had never played tennis much but loved the sport so took it up that spring. I used to hit the ball into the air and see how many times I could hit it without it falling to the ground. That was a good coordination exercise for learning tennis. I tried most of the sports offered at Wichita University, including modern dancing. That was the one thing I did not like, but had to take it and be in one recital for my physical education minor. I was not the graceful, flowing figure and it was not my style but I did it.

My first year of college was behind me now and I was establishing a name for myself in sports, if not in the classroom. One of the things I liked best about college was the privilege of cutting three classes in each subject per semester. I didn't cut many PE classes, of course, but did cut Shakespeare, education classes, and other dull subjects to the maximum. It was the freedom to cut if you wanted to that appealed to me.

Wichita University had about 1500 students enrolled, so you got to know most of the students and professors. Many of the professors from my era later had buildings named after them. Dr. Jardine was president, Grace Wilke was dean of women, Thurlow Lieurance was head of fine arts, Frank Neff was dean of business administration and Isley, Wilner, and Duerkson were some of the profs who had buildings named after them. To the new students, they are just names. To us old-timers, they were personalities.

I did not join a sorority, but was a member of the Vandals, an independent group. I felt that I could be friends with all the sororities if I was independent and was always glad I made that decision. I thought the sorority members were restricted in their social life. Besides, I was more interested in sports than in social life.

It was now time to get ready for a fifth season with our carnival in Colorado. I never tired of seeing those beautiful mountains. In the spring, my dreams were of going west again.

COLLEGE YEARS

FLYING AND RIFLE

The summer of 1938 was fairly routine. Our carnival business was very good and we had many visitors from Wichita during the summer. We were rained out a lot less than usual and had a good location. We apparently did not take a Colorado trip after closing and headed right back for Wichita. I started taking care of Benny Benjamin again as soon as I got back. School started at Wichita University and the whirlwind of activity had begun.

Eddie Ottaway, Herb's brother, had bought a 40-horsepower Cub airplane and was keeping it at the National Guard hangar on the east side of municipal airport. The plane had no rear wheel, only a tail skid, so it was hard to taxi in a wind, especially as there were no concrete runways at that time. One day in October he asked me to take a ride and let me take the controls. After he took over the controls again, we did loops and spins and had a great time. It was then that I decided I wanted to learn how to fly.

I saved up my baby-sitting money until I had enough to fly an hour. Eddie charged me $2 an hour for lessons, which included gasoline and instructor. I made my first solo flight off municipal field on December 27, the day after my 19th birthday. Lloyd McJunkin came out to solo me, as Eddie had only a student permit and wasn't qualified, at least on paper. Sam Arnholz, Dad's boss, had a movie camera and came out to record this important event. Mom and Dad came, as did Lloyd and Eddie. I remember making a big wide pattern so I made a long straight-in approach. I made three landings and take-offs and was quite excited about the whole thing.

After five hours of solo, we were required to get a solo license. These were discontinued shortly after I got mine so it really didn't accomplish anything. Solo pilots were still not allowed to take up passengers but the Civil Aeronautics Authority did not enforce that rule very well. I was taking my dad for rides before I had very many solo hours. Dad and I were flying back from Albert Ottaway's farm at Goddard one day and the engine started heating up. We made a forced landing north of town when it was just farmland. The plane had run out of oil, so Dad went up to a farm house and used their phone to call Eddie. Eddie flew over in another airplane with some oil and we were off and flying again.

When spring came, I was trying out for the Kemper rifle team again and this year made it. This was an exciting experience, going to a military school, attending the military ball, shooting under stress, having fun with my teammates, and staying in a grand old hotel. As the only left-handed shooter at the meet I used up two shooting slots in the prone position. This was because I was lying at a ninety degree angle to the right-handers, with my feet sticking into the next space. I did get a 100 (possible) target in competition this year. We shot both individual and team targets. We were there only two days, but they were fun-filled. In the three years that I attended the meet, Wichita University won either first or second place.

School was soon out and it was off to Colorado for our sixth season. Things were pretty routine in both instances. I was starting to build up some flying time and was loving it more all the time. At the end of the season in Colorado, we took a trip to the Ozarks. I saw my first major league baseball game in St. Louis. Bob Feller, famous fastball pitcher with Cleveland, beat the St. Louis Browns. As I remember, there were only about 400 people attending this game. We went to Lindbergh Field and I took a half-hour of dual flight time at night. We went to Bagnel Dam and visited several towns in Missouri including Springfield, Buffalo, and Joplin. I think this was the farthest east I had ever been.

Shortly after school started, I heard about a Civilian Pilot Training course being offered at the University, so I went to see if I could get in. The limit was 30 students and there were already 30 boys enrolled by the time I heard about it. However, I checked every day with the man in charge to see if any boys had dropped out. Finally, just before the course started, one boy did drop out and I was in. Since I was the only girl, I got lots of publicity in the Sunflower (the school paper) and the Wichita papers. Lloyd McJunkin, the man who had soloed me, was my flight instructor. He was quite tough on me but told me later that he had to be tough as all eyes were on me as the only girl. This was an exciting time as I would have my private pilot's license when I finished the course.

This group formed the Flying Shockers Club. The fellows all wore white coveralls and I wore a white gabardine skirt and jacket that my sister made for me. We started out with the ground school, then started flying second semester. I remember one day I was scheduled to fly, so wore my uniform. When I got to the airport, the instructor informed me that I was going to have to wear a parachute that day as we were going to do aerobatics. Well, it was quite embarrassing to have to strap up both legs with a skirt on but I did. I think they had plotted to do this, just to harass the "token female."

My examiner for my private license was Billy Carpenter, who ran a flying service out of Winfield, about 30 miles southeast of Wichita. I flew down to take the flight test and was doing well until we climbed to about 2,000 feet to do stalls and spins. It was June by this time and the weather was warm enough. However, after turning on the carburetor heat before throttling back, the engine quit. This was quite a predicament since we had no starter in the plane. Billy took over and did a wing-over type maneuver to get the propeller to windmill. It turned out to be successful, so we didn't have to make a forced landing. I thought I had surely flunked the test, but I guess he was so glad to get down safely that he passed me.

With my private license in hand, it was off to Colorado again. It was 1940 now and in one more year I would graduate from Wichita University. I was well on my way to accomplishing my goal of being a gym teacher but flying had now become the most important thing in my life. I rented a plane in Colorado Springs to take my friends and relatives up. We flew off a farm just southeast of Colorado Springs that was owned by the grandparents of big Al Unser, the famous race car driver. This was the summer that all the Montana cousins (about 10 of them) came down and I took them all for a ride over Manitou, one at a time. I think it took most of the day.

A senior at Wichita University, at last. I had thoroughly enjoyed my last three years and was looking forward to my best year yet. I continued to build up flying time off the campus and was still involved in many sports. The Women's Recreation Association, of which I was president, had a convention in Albuquerque so four of us drove out, with mother as chaperone. The University of New Mexico, with its Indian motif, was beautiful. We sampled real Mexican food, saw a lot of sights, and met girls from all over the region who also were active in sports and recreation.

By now, the university had moved the rifle range to the basement of the commons building. This was much easier than climbing four flights of stairs and putting up with the wind tunnel. I made the Kemper team for the third year and, as usual, we had a real "bang up" time. We won the first place trophy and presented it to President Jardine. I was honored by the Blue Key, an honor fraternity. Fifteen senior women who had been outstanding in athletics, debate and dramatics were honored at a banquet in the spring. I was selected for my rifle activities. The speaker at the banquet was "Phogg" Allen, of Kansas University basketball fame.

We had a May Fete and one of the events was for the Worst Dressed on Campus. I think I was the only girl who entered, so naturally I won. I had a lot of fun dressing up in a gunny sack, an old shirt and tennis shoes, and got my picture in the annual in that costume. I was also pictured many times on the sports pages and once as a Flying Shocker. You can see that I didn't make the "brainy" page, but I did well enough to graduate with above-average grades. We weren't required to attend our graduation. I really can't remember attending it, so I probably didn't go. I still didn't like to dress up.

We went to Manitou for the last summer. By this time, Harold and I were both dating and gave Mom a hard time. We would rather be having fun than working. The reason for us going to Colorado had been accomplished. I had finished college and had been hired to teach English (and a lot of other things) in the small town of Ford, Kansas.

I had hoped for a physical education job, but taught mostly English, dramatics, journalism, and geometry, was sponsor for the cheer leaders, and taught P.E. two hours a week. All this for $90 a month, but I got room and breakfast for $9 a month and meals at the local cafe were 50 cents each. I had no car and other than buying a few clothes, had no other expenses so I managed to save money with this salary.

I didn't have any trouble adjusting to being on my own as we had learned a lot about getting along frugally as we were growing up and in managing the carnival in Colorado so many summers. In those days, there was very little credit, so if we didn't have the money, we didn't spend it. Young people would be better off today if credit weren't so readily available.

TEACHING AT FORD, KANSAS

Ford was a typical small farming community about 18 miles east of Dodge City in western Kansas. I had been through there many times as it was on our way to Colorado. If you blink, you might miss it. The main drag was highway 154 and the greater downtown area was about two blocks long. A drug store, grocery store, and cafe were on the west side of the street. Across the street was the local post office, a very popular place. In the block to the south was the telephone office. We had phones that you had to crank to get Central. A lady answered the switchboard 24 hours a day. Of course, everybody knew when somebody rang in, so there was no privacy on a telephone line. How else were they going to be entertained in this small town?

A city park and a community building were across the street from this block. Ford had only about 400 residents, but it supported a high school and a grade school, a grain elevator, a railroad depot, and several churches. The Arkansas River actually flowed north of Ford during this time but it has been a long time since it has been more than a trickle. Colorado built a reservoir in the 1930s and there has been a fight over the water ever since then. So far, Kansas has been the loser.

There were about 80 students in the high school, some of whom were bussed in from up to 10 miles away. Agriculture was a very popular subject in school. There were a lot of good, honest, hard-working people in this town, but they were very conservative. They expected their teachers to be very straight-laced and I'm afraid I didn't fit the pattern. Between the time they hired me and when I showed up in late August, I had acquired quite a reputation. They heard I was in Colorado with our little carnival and that put me in a very rough crowd. They heard I flew airplanes and rode motorcycles and I'm sure those stories got out of hand. However I came and continued to do the things I loved and they found out I was pretty normal after all.

My English room on the third floor had a good view out the windows on the east and was a great observation point for the athletic field. The pencil sharpener was also by the windows, and it is amazing how many pencils had to be sharpened, and sharpened, and sharpened.

I had one freshman named Donnie who wasn't very studious but had a great sense of humor. In fact, the whole family did. Donnie insisted on chewing on his pencil and I tried to get him to break the habit. I promised him a reward if he would not do it. Every day he would show me his pencil without teeth marks on it and I would compliment him. It finally dawned on me that he was showing me his extra pencil and his habit persisted.

I lived with a Mrs. Patterson about four blocks from the school in the south end of town. She also kept the home economics teacher, who was the ideal conservative lady that the school board liked, very nice but quite dull. Mrs. Patterson was a Nazarene and religion was her life.

Her daughter and family, the Arthur Powells, lived across the street to the south of her. They had two children, Dean (a junior in high school) and Ramona, a sixth-grader. Dean was a bright, mischievous boy. He and I played a lot of tennis on the courts that were about two blocks from his house. I think some of the school board frowned on this as I would play in my shorts and many times on Sundays but we didn't let it interfere with our tennis games. He was planning to join the Navy after he was out of school and was learning Morse code. I wanted to learn Morse code also as it was recommended for pilots. So we got flashlights and flashed codes across the street from his house to his grandmother's house, where I lived.

Ramona, though quite young, was a pianist and a great girl to be around. She and I are still good friends after all these years. The family had a player piano, which was lots of fun. Mr. Powell was a farmer and a rural mail carrier. He had wonderful gardens, the biggest sunflowers I have ever seen, and Ethel did a lot of canning and was a super cook. Dean did join the Navy and became a career sailor. I had lots of friends in Ford, but the Powell family was always special. I took all of them flying from Ethel's sister's farm. This was the first family after I left home that became my second family. Wherever I went, God put me with fine, loving people.

Jim Heiland and his wife ran the local cafe. You can't imagine the good and plentiful food we got for 50 cents. All the teachers ate there and the camaraderie was great. The math teacher married one of her students at mid-term so couldn't teach any more. The board members didn't give that marriage a chance, but I saw them at the 1995 reunion and they had celebrated 53 years of wedded bliss. I took over her geometry classes and was given a $10 raise, giving me a total of $100 per month.

I would ride the bus to Wichita for a visit about once a month. It seems the wind was always blowing a gale when I came back late at night. I had about a four-block walk, but nobody worried about being out in this little town. A bunch of the kids and teachers would often play run-sheep-run in the neighborhoods in the evenings. We rode bikes and played a lot of tennis. Once the river flooded and we all rode our bikes out to see the damage. I dated several fellows during this time and we would take in shows in Dodge City or other towns around. I liked to go hunting with Donnie's brothers and we did a lot of things that didn't cost anything.

I visited Dodge City a lot as that was the closest large town. One of Dad's "character" friends, Mac Stauffer, lived in Dodge so I looked him up quite often. He had a motorcycle shop that was so crowded with parts, tools and just plain stuff you could hardly get through it. He was always dressed in black (boots, shirt, and jodhpurs). I am not sure if he ever washed them — or himself. The rumor was that he wore black because he had been driving the car in which his wife and daughter were killed in an accident. He had been a motorcycle rider, promoter, and racer. I doubt there was a person around who didn't know Mac Stauffer.

I had started dating Frank Litton in Colorado Springs in 1941, the last summer we had our carnival. He was Harold's good friend and I had become good friends with him and all his family. I took a train out to the Springs once or twice that year to visit them. Frank's sister's family owned a potato chip factory. Years later we took my daughters through the factory when the younger one was about three years old. She had a ball picking up all the chips off the floor. She thought she had died and gone to potato chip heaven until we stopped her.

One Sunday afternoon we were all downtown listening to our car radios when the dreadful news blasted out that the Japanese had bombed Pearl Harbor. It was December 7, 1941. We were all in shock and knew at that moment that our world had changed.

Frank and I dated and corresponded until 1944, when he was listed as missing in action after a B17 mission to Germany. I remained good friends with his family for many years. Mrs. Litton died after the age of 90, never knowing what had happened to Frank.

My first year of teaching was coming to an end and I came to a crossroads in my career. The school officials weren't sure about my life style, despite my church activities and my being very conscientious about teaching. Nor was I sure I wanted to come back. About that time, I read about opportunities for women in air traffic control. The men were being drafted and the Civil Aeronautics Authority needed to train women and get the air traffic control system in full gear. I did enjoy my first year of teaching but was anxious to get into something related to aviation and this seemed like a good chance.

As I met their qualifications — a pilot's license and a college degree — I sent my application to Kansas City and shortly was asked to come there for an interview. It was about April when I took the train from Dodge City to Kansas City. I was hired immediately and went to work in the Airway Traffic Control Center in Denver on June 1, 1942. I had never heard of airway traffic control and had no experience until I took on-the-job training. Two other girls and I were the only ones to be trained on the job, as they quickly set up training centers for those coming along later.

AIR TRAFFIC CONTROL AT DENVER

After the school year was over at Ford, I returned to Wichita to gather all my worldly possessions into two suitcases and took the Missouri Pacific train to Denver. It was June 1, 1942, and I was off to a new career. I had no idea what the job in the Airway Traffic Control Center (ATC) was all about, had no place to stay, no transportation, and no acquaintances in Denver except Uncle Bob. He lived on the west side of Denver and I wanted to settle on the east side near the airport. I don't remember having any qualms about heading out there alone, but looked forward to being in aviation instead of teaching.

From the train depot in Denver, I got on a streetcar that went east toward the airport to look for a place to live. Along the way, I saw a sign in the window of a realty company for a place that had room and board and got off to check. Just that morning a family had advertised with this company and the room was still open, so I walked to their home, which was only a block down the street. Bill and Rose McEnulty and their three daughters, Mary, Rita, and Ann, greeted me with open arms and we remained life-long friends. They were the second family to take me under their wing and become my "adopted family." How lucky could I be!

I am surprised they didn't kick me out after the first night, though. I had periodically walked in my sleep and did so that night, busily rearranging the furniture in my downstairs bedroom. They had a great sense of humor, however, and we all had a big laugh about it.

Life was never dull at the McEnulty home. They were a Catholic family and went to mass nearly every morning. The McEnulty girls were all in school and slept upstairs. Mary was about 17 and very studious. She went to nurses training after high school so didn't live at home after graduation. She later married and had seven children. Rita was about 15 when I arrived and a very beautiful girl. She went on to college, married and also had seven children. Ann was about 12 at that time and a cute little tomboy. She married when she was 18, had a baby boy, then died of bulbar polio on her 19th birthday. I was driving to Denver on a vacation when I stopped at a restaurant and saw the headlines and Ann's picture on the front page of the Rocky Mountain News. It was a great shock and so very sad.

Mr. Mac went elk hunting every fall and for the most part that was what we ate all winter long. He sat at the head of the table with all the plates and served us, then passed the plates around. Mr. Mac loved to garden and we all especially enjoyed the huge strawberries he produced. He worked for the State of Colorado downtown and took the streetcar down and back every day. I am not sure they had a car at that time. Even if they did, gas was rationed so they used public transportation all they could. Mrs. Mac fixed our lunches to take to work or school. As I remember, it was usually peanut butter sandwiches.

One time, for a joke they got a contraption and put it under my plate. It was connected to a bulb that they would squeeze and make my plate move. I kept thinking it was my imagination and didn't say anything for a while. Then I said, "my plate is moving." They assured me it was my imagination. They were all about to bust out laughing when I finally discovered the contraption under my plate. There were many more fun times at the table. I remember the first time they came to the breakfast table with dirty foreheads. I had no idea what that was all about until they explained Ash Wednesday to me.

Within a month, Joyce Mead and Madelyn Brown became the second and third females to arrive at the ATC. Madelyn, a teacher from Missouri, told me that she was not feeling very well as she had just had her tonsils out, was homesick, and wondered how she had gotten into this mess. She said she had no place to live and I assured her that the McEnultys would probably take her in. Well, they did and she fit right into the family, becoming the second ATC gal to join the McEnulty clan. She was a beautiful blonde and very popular at work and at the Macs'. When I saw her a couple of years ago, she was still beautiful, still a great person, and said she is in debt to me for getting her a place to stay and a second family to cure her homesickness.

71

The third ATC gal to move in with the Macs was Marge Haynes who, along with Madelyn, remained my life-long friend. She was also a lot of fun and a pretty girl. The Macs had to fix up their attic into sort of a dorm for Madelyn and Marge. I spent a lot of time there, but remained in "The Queen's Bedroom" downstairs.

That household was ringing with laughter most of the time. It must have been a nightmare to try to keep track of us, as well as the McEnulty girls who had all their school and social activities also. With a wife and six other females, I don't know how Mr. Mac put up with it but he seemed to enjoy it. I do not ever remember the house being locked nor do I remember having a key to the house.

Our first job in the center was on the "B" stand, a glorified telephone operator's job. We wore headsets and talked to air bases, flight stations, airline operators, and others who filed flight plans. We got pretty fast at taking down the data and passing it over to the "A" boards where all the information was plotted on strips of paper and the controllers would maintain separation of all the aircraft on the airways until the flights were turned over to the towers for landing clearance. After we had been there a short time, we worked on the "A" boards under supervision for a few months before they turned us loose.

There were 12 male controllers when I showed up and if they resented having women in their midst, they didn't show it. We women all did our jobs as well as possible and didn't try to outdo the men so I think we earned their respect. They teased me about being from Kansas, however, saying there were no dogs in Kansas as there were no trees, and other such remarks. The fellows and their wives became our good friends. We had a lot of get-togethers, picnics in the mountains and other social events.

We changed shifts every week, so we worked an eight-hour daylight shift for a week at a time, then an evening shift for the next week, and on to a hoot-owl shift. And around it went. This made it difficult to ever get used to sleeping, but we were young and survived.

I got to and from work by riding with the other controllers, taking the bus, riding a bike borrowed from Ann McEnulty, or walking.

In those days, we had no fear of walking home alone at midnight. We lived only about a mile from the airport, so it took about 20 or 30 minutes to get there. The other controllers didn't seem to mind picking us up and we would share our gas ration coupons with them. Later, I started dating one of the controllers, John Rupp, and rode with him a lot if we were working the same shift.

The administration building was very small by today's standards. It had a lobby, office space, and a restaurant on the first floor. The Airway Traffic Control Center was up one flight of stairs (no elevator), along with the weather bureau and the radio communications station with all its teletype machines. (I always marveled at how they could read their ticker tape. We had learned to read the weather symbols and other aircraft reports, but not the ticker tape.) Then the control tower was up another flight of stairs. That was about it.

Things were certainly different then. In those days all the planes were tail-draggers. That is, they dragged their tail ends on a small rear wheel. Tricycle gears, which keep the planes almost level when on the ground, didn't come about for another year or two. Radios in planes weren't required to land at the big airports. The tower personnel announced the arrival of airline flights. We had a microphone that activated when we picked it up and deactivated when we set it down. Once in a while, we would set it down on a piece of paper or something and found ourselves unintentionally broadcasting all over the building.

Air traffic was heavy, especially with all the military planes in the area. Sometimes, the Army fields would just tell us how many planes they would have off their fields and their expected take-off and landing times. Not much control there, but we were aware of them and warned other traffic about them. This was the time before radar and I always wondered if the pilots' reports were very accurate. They could tell us they were at an altitude of 12,000 feet at a certain time, but we had no proof of it. However, I remember no incidents or close calls on the airways.

In the meantime, I continued to fly and didn't waste much time getting my commercial pilot's license. Contrary to what many people believe, the commercial license allowed you to fly for pay, rather than for the airlines. (That required an airline transport rating, a multi-engine rating, and much more than the 200 hours flying time needed

73

for a commercial.) I studied for the written test and, flying a Luscombe most of the time, worked on all the maneuvers that were required and received my commercial in 1943.

After about six months in the Center, I was promoted to the Denver tower as an assistant controller. I loved the action in the tower much better than in the Center. I was there for another six months and then had to go back to the Center for some additional training. I guess I spent another six months down there before I was promoted back to the Denver tower as a full controller. I never wanted to go back to the Center, even for more training for another promotion, so this is as high as I went in air traffic control. I became a controller about the same time I got my commercial pilot's license.

In early 1944, I decided I wanted a transfer to the Wichita tower. I guess I was kind of homesick and wanted to get back to my home town. My trip back to Wichita in March was one to remember. I had purchased my first car, a 1938 Chevy and kind of a junker. It had started snowing that morning in Denver and my car had frozen up. After getting it thawed out, I put my belongings in the car and started out about noon.

I headed east toward Limon and the slush kept building up under the fenders so I could hardly turn the wheels and the brakes froze up. I stopped at a garage in Limon and they tried to help but didn't do much good. Since I was already late getting started, I took off toward the south through the God-forsaken eastern Colorado desert country. The snow storm intensified and darkness set in as I drove south with no brakes and not much ability to turn.

To this day, I don't see how I stayed on the road. It was snowing so hard it almost hypnotized me as the snow blew into the head-lights. I knew if I stopped, I would never go on and nobody else was on the road that night. I could see no lights from houses, so I just kept driving and miraculously stayed on the road. I breathed a sigh of relief when I came to the road to Lamar. I put the car in a garage, hoping the ice would melt as I slept, but it didn't.

The next day, I headed east toward Kansas. So far, so good — until I tried to turn a corner at Dodge City and the car wouldn't turn. I hit the back fender of a pickup, gave the owner $10 for his damage, then went on another 18 miles to Ford where my friends lived. Mr. Powell worked on getting the brakes thawed out and the fenders clear. The rest of the trip was a breeze.

My folks were astounded that I would start out in that storm. I admit it wasn't too smart and I was, again, VERY LUCKY!

WICHITA AND HUTCHINSON TOWERS

After my grueling trip to Wichita, I moved back home with my folks. Dad was still working for Arnholz Coffee Company and Mom was busy with her church work and taking care of Dad and all his friends. There was a constant stream of visitors when Dad was home. By now he had acquired quite a collection of antique cars and motorcycles that were in various stages of restoration. Some were in boxes and others had been restored to A-1 condition. He had built a shop at the back of the property where he restored them and rented a garage across the street where he kept his extra "choice plunder" as he called it. It looked like junk to me.

Our house had always been the gathering spot in all the neighborhoods we lived in. Dad loved the front porch swing and the porch was the gathering spot for visitors and neighbors who dropped by. He was a most interesting person and Mom a cordial hostess.

My new post was at the municipal airport in Wichita. The building was started in 1930, boarded up when half-finished due to the Depression, then finished in 1935. It is a lovely building with Art Deco designs reflecting aviation and the Indian heritage of the area. A large cast-stone mural over the front door depicts Charles Lindbergh approaching the European continent after his 1927 flight. The building is now on the National Register of Historic Places and houses the Kansas Aviation Museum. The museum certainly has a lot of aviation heritage to preserve, as Kansans began flying and building planes as early as 1910 and have been at it ever since. There is a good reason Wichita calls itself Air Capital of the World as more airplanes have been built there than anywhere else in the world.

During my stint in the Wichita tower, I helped train a lot of assistant controllers who had been to the formal classes. My memories of this time are vivid: Kay who taught me how to knit (no small trick for a right-hander to teach a lefty), Woody who first worked in the city tower, Tom who was the best controller in the tower, John who was chief of the tower and whom we all liked, and especially the camaraderie among a close-knit group of people.

Very soon after I came back to Wichita, I started working on my flight instructor rating under Dot Lemon on the municipal field. We were probably flying out of Harte Flying Service. I received my rating in November of 1944. I can't remember much about this part of my flying career, so it must have been pretty routine.

Sometime in 1944 I was sent to the tower in Hutchinson, a smaller nearby town, against my wishes. I did not like it over there as the air traffic was very slow. We had a chief who was most unpopular. Apparently he was pretty impressed with himself for being a chief, even though it was at an unimportant little airport. One runway was under construction and about the only airplanes flying were the Cessna Bobcats that were being manufactured there. Many planes did not have radios, so we got quite adept with the light gun. This was a gizmo that we used to flash a red or green light at the planes so the pilots would know whether they could land or take off.

The Hutchinson tower was a free-standing wooden structure with outside stairs. We abandoned this tower several times when winds were over 80 mph. However, the tower was never damaged by winds and it was finally torn down when the new tower was built on the administration building.

Since we had very little traffic, I would turn on the regular broadcast band and listen to music. The chief would hear the music in his room just below us and come up and turn it off. As soon as he was back downstairs, I would turn it on again. Sort of a battle of wills. Also, the midnight shift had almost zero traffic, so we decided to bring our cots up so we could sleep. He frowned on that also. One day, after about four months of this, I decided that if this was the best I could do, I didn't want to stay in air traffic control. I walked out and went back to Wichita.

After about a week, John, the tower chief in Wichita, called me in for a talk. I was hired back into the Wichita tower and was on probation for about six months. John would dutifully call me in once a month for my regular report, but we both knew there was no real problem since I was back in Wichita.

While I was still in Hutchinson, I got my first decent car, a 1940 Mercury coupe. I was so proud of this car and kept it washed and polished but it developed a problem that nobody ever solved. The lights would go out while I was driving and then would come back on. It happened on the highway, in the mountains, and at various other inopportune times. I took it to many repair shops, but it was never fixed. It is a wonder that I didn't have an accident when that happened. Just lucky again!

After getting back to Wichita, I started making use of my instructor's rating, teaching several fellow controllers to fly, often in an Aeronca I rented from Bill Nichols. We flew off the municipal runways and used an auxiliary field just southeast of the airport to practice landings. The Aeronca was a sweet little plane but had a lot of dihedral in its wings. That meant that the wings angled up slightly from the fuselage, so it was particularly susceptible to being blown over by a cross-wind.

One day, Bill chided us for not wanting to fly the Aeronca in the wind, so one of my students, Corrine Schultz, and I thought we'd show him. The wind was probably blowing about 30 with gusts, but we took off with no problem. After flying a while we returned to municipal, got clearance to land to the west, acknowledged by wiggling our wings as our radio had a receiver only, and made a good landing right in front of the tower.

But we had heard the tower clear a TWA plane to land behind us, so knew we had better get off the runway as soon as possible. We also knew that, with the winds as strong as they were, we might be blown over as soon as we turned cross-wind. We had no choice, however, and sure enough, after turning off the runway, we were spun into a 360-degree turn and back into the wind. In spinning around, we dragged a wing tip and broke the tail wheel. A very embarrassing thing to do in front of your friends in the tower.

Another time, Corrine (who also was a controller) and I had been working the day shift and decided to fly to Kansas City to visit our friends in that tower. She had never flown at night and I had had very little experience, but we took off with all the confidence in the world. We still had only a receiver in the plane, so couldn't talk to the tower. We arrived at Kansas City after dark and were immediately confused about how to taxi to the ramp. They led us in on our radio, but it wasn't easy to find all the right taxi-ways, making for a very worrisome situation.

We visited friends in the tower for a while, then decided to take a streetcar down to the Airway Traffic Control Center and visit other friends. About 3 a.m. we got back on another street car and rode all over Kansas City, just to kill time so we could fly back with a little daylight. As I remember, we got back to Wichita in time to work another day shift. We must have been real sharp that day!

Bill Nichols started giving me instruction for my instrument rating in 1945. At first I flew his Taylorcraft and finished up in his Curtiss Robin. The Curtiss Robin was very noisy and clumsy to fly, and it was quite hard to hear radio signals in it. During this time, the only navigational aids were a compass, gyro, and the old A & N radio signals. With these signals, you would get a monotone if you were on the beam. If you varied to the left or right, you would get either an A or N signal, which were dot-dash and dash-dot. There were approach and departure patterns to learn while we were trying to hear these signals. I can remember counting one-and, two-and, etc. in keeping track of the seconds you were flying a certain direction. All the time you had to hold your altitude. Compared to today's procedures, it took a lot of concentration. Bill was a tough instructor, but I got my rating in May, 1945.

We had lots of interesting traffic while I was working in the Wichita tower, including B29s and Culver PQ14s. We had some exciting times — from near-misses to the tower windows blowing out to a major fire — and also some very dull moments when the weather was socked in or when there were very few flights during the middle of the night.

However, this was a very active time for Wichita with all the manufacturing going at full speed for the war effort. Beech, Cessna, Boeing, and Culver were all producing planes during the war. Boeing was adjacent to municipal airport and used our field exclusively for all flights in and out of the factory, as well as for all their test flying. Others conducted glider flights as well as helicopter flights off the field. Several flying schools were operating out of our field, trying to train all the pilots they could for the war effort. We also had a variety of types of planes and air speeds to contend with. This made for an interesting mix of traffic.

An incident with a B29 gave me my biggest scare. At that time there were dual north-south runways, a southeast-northwest runway, and two east-west runways on the field. The B29s were not allowed to take off northwest over the little settlement of Plainview but had to take off to the north. The runways intersected in the middle of the field, which could be a real problem when we had northwest traffic.

One day when we did have northwest traffic, there were six or seven planes lined up to land and I had two B29s holding for a north take-off. Since the landing craft always had the right-of-way, the B29s were both waiting for a break. Suddenly one B29 took off without clearance. I radioed for him to hold, but by the time he got stopped, he had already rolled past the intersection. Fortunately, there was no collision but it sure gave me a headache. The commanding officer was in the pattern at the time and heard and saw the whole thing. The tower was not in trouble, but I think the B29 pilot was.

The PQ14s were pesky little planes, one-seaters without radios. They were sort of like mosquitoes — just flitting around. Sometimes the factory told us when they were coming, but more often they just showed up in the pattern, usually six or eight at a time. We got a lot more experience on the light gun with them.

Then there was the night that a group of B25s arrived in the pattern. They were flown by Chinese pilots who were being trained in New Mexico and were on a navigation training mission. A Chinese interpreter had been sent to the tower, but he couldn't understand our instructions and the Chinese pilots spoke no English. So, we told all other traffic to hold clear of the field until the B25s were on the ground and turned the microphone over to the interpreter. I will never forget the babble of sounds on the airwaves that evening.

The day the windows blew out of the tower had been a wild weather day. The winds and the rain would hit us from the northwest, then the storms would turn around and come back in from the east with winds gusting up to 70 to 80 m.p.h. many times. All day we had been ducking behind the radio receiver racks whenever a big gust would hit us. The windows sounded as if they were going to blow out, so in the afternoon we called a man to tighten them. This man was sitting on the ledge above the stairway working on the windows when somebody opened a door and the sudden change in air pressure took out the windows. We all ducked at the same time. Fortunately, since the glass all blew outward, none of us was cut. At a reunion in 1992, one of the controllers, said, "You know, I landed on top of you." I don't remember that, but I guess that shows I was faster than he was.

The most spectacular event of my career in the Wichita tower happened September 25, 1945. Our tower chief, John Claar, was in Kansas City on official business and many controllers were ill, so I was working alone on the 3-11 p.m. shift. The weather was below minimums for CFR (contact flight rules) flights. This meant all planes had to have an IFR (instruments flight rules) clearance. In these conditions you have a lot more involvement with each plane. All traffic must be on a flight plan and all this had to be coordinated with the control center in Kansas City.

To complicate matters, a Continental plane had requested to land to the south when traffic was to the southeast. Since I was alone and the runways crossed, I could not allow him to land south. I was facing the northwest, watching the planes approach for a southeast landing and looked back on the field only to see the Continental had landed south without clearance. I had to write a violation on him (the only one I remember writing).

Charlie Straub, the airport manager, had been up to the tower helping me answer phones while I was so busy. Things finally settled down and Charlie left.

Then, about 9 p.m., a Braniff on the ramp reported over the radio that there was a fire in our hangar about 100 yards east of the tower! He asked for a quick take-off so he wouldn't be involved as things heated up. I had noticed the fire just as the Braniff reported it to me. When an emergency occurred, we had a list of procedures to follow and people to call. The first thing was to sound the airport siren to alert anybody nearby that something was wrong. Then I was to call the hangar directly to get the airport fire department. Since the fire engine was in the front part of the hangar, I knew they couldn't get it out, so I didn't call them. But I did call the Boeing fire department, then the Wichita department. Soon there were a lot of fire engines on the scene.

Next I tried to call Charlie Straub but he did not answer. He told me later that he was just arriving home with his family and heard the sirens and the phone and knew it was at the airport, so he just took off. He worked tirelessly for about three days. Then I called my chief in Kansas City and others who needed to be informed. Then the phones went out, next the power went out in the building as well as the runway lights. It was necessary to close the field at that time. Naturally, I had an Army plane that was scheduled to come in. He was very insistent on landing in Wichita, despite the fact that the airport was closed. It took an order from his commanding officer to divert him to another airport.

When the power went off in the building, we had to go on auxiliary power. When we turned on auxiliary power, we were supposed to open a window in the basement where the motor was, so it wouldn't overheat but since I was the only one on duty, I couldn't leave the tower. The roads soon jammed with traffic to the airport so my relief controller had great difficulty getting to work. When he finally arrived, I immediately sent him to take care of the motor in the basement. Then I watched with great sadness as that beautiful hangar, 27 airplanes, and one fire engine burned that night. Fortunately, nobody was injured. The hangar was never rebuilt.

CHEYENNE TOWER

While I was working in the Wichita tower, I started dating Marion Neary, a radio installation employee for the Civil Aeronautics Authority. He was a pilot, a tennis player, and a lot of fun to be with. Marion was thin and over six feet tall and I stood at five feet two inches so he and I were a little like Mutt and Jeff. He was transferred to Laramie, Wyoming in 1945. To be near him, I asked for a transfer to Cheyenne tower and arrived there in December 1945.

I knew several of the tower operators in Cheyenne, which eased the shock of going to a strange place. Don Murphy, the chief, had been in the Wichita tower before I came and had married one of my high school friends. Three of the gals were friends from Denver. And, as I said, I was dating Marion Neary and he was the reason I transferred to Cheyenne.

When I first moved to Cheyenne I lived in a basement apartment that was a depressing hole. I soon moved to a second story apartment where I stayed the rest of my time out there. Shortly after arriving, I put an ad in the newspaper for someone to play tennis with. You would never do that in this day and age. The man who answered my ad was a Mr. Shanafelt (Shanny) who was 56 years old. I was only 25 at the time, so he seemed very old to me. He met me at the tennis courts and introduced me to most of the people who regularly played tennis in Cheyenne. One girl I played with was Evelyn Bernica. She was the best female player in town and taught me a lot. We won the city doubles title in 1946 and she was the singles champion. I met a whole new circle of friends and we often went at Shanny's house to play Ping-Pong and have get-togethers.

One of the gals from Denver, Virginia (Mac) MacCracken, and I had a bit of trouble over the initials we signed our logs with. I had used MC since starting in Denver. She used CM until she transferred to Cheyenne, then she changed to MC. When I came, she had priority as she was in Cheyenne first. It was really hard to change after four years. We were still good friends, but I think I resented her making me change my initials.

Mac went on to be one of the first three female Senior Airway Traffic controllers in the country. She stayed in ATC until she retired and we corresponded at Christmas time all our lives. She loved to take cruises and go on exotic vacations. She never married but took care of her mother. Shortly after her mother's death, Mac developed cancer and died in 1991. It didn't seem fair that she should have met that fate, just as she was free to travel again. She surely must have a crown in heaven for her devotion. She was loved by all the controllers and spent her last working years in the center where she started.

A lot of exciting incidents happened while I was working in the tower in Cheyenne. Airline traffic was fairly heavy and we had Army traffic along with private flying. We really laughed one time when a pilot, working alone, spun the propeller on his plane one morning. He had apparently set the throttle a little high and the plane started taxiing by itself. The pilot took off in hot pursuit, chasing it all over the ramp. Apparently he eventually caught it but I am betting that was the last time he started an airplane without somebody being in the cockpit to control it.

The atmosphere out there was such that we kept losing sight of aircraft in the pattern. Cheyenne was very windy and this produced a dusty, hazy condition so the planes blended in with the sky. The east end of the east-west runway was at least a mile from the tower. At that distance, we often had to tell the pilots to wiggle their wings so we could see them.

One day a twin-engine Beech was on final approach east of the east-west runway and cleared to land. I looked away for a few seconds and when I looked back, I couldn't find him anywhere. I grabbed the field glasses to see if he was on the runway, but he was nowhere to be found and he didn't respond to radio calls. I asked a Continental airliner coming into the pattern to look for the Beech. Continental spotted him in a low spot off the end of the runway. When the Beech was on final, he pulled the wrong lever and lost all power. He pancaked in short of the runway. No injuries, but damaged props and embarrassed pilots. I was a bit embarrassed for losing him from sight.

I witnessed my only major airplane crash in nearly five years of control tower work in about November of 1946. It happened on the night shift. A United DC4 passenger plane arriving from the west coast had been cleared to make an instrument approach. Weather was below instrument flying minimums, with poor visibility and actual ceiling below 400 feet. In those conditions, the ATC procedure was to fly a pattern and break out of the clouds heading west over the east-west runway. If they didn't break out of the clouds by the time they were 400 feet above the ground, they were to do a missed approach and try again or fly to their alternate airport.

The second time the United pilot broke out just in front of the tower and not more than 200 feet above the ground. He started a slow left turn to make a pattern to land southeast. He made the bend left, then a slow right turn to head for his base leg. As he was making his turn near the Cheyenne Rodeo Stadium, his wing tip hit the ground and he crashed.

The emergency equipment and all other necessary personnel quickly raced to the crash scene. From the tower we saw only a ball of fire and just knew all aboard were killed. Fortunately, only two people sitting over the wing died. I called United in Denver on a direct line as we reported to them when their planes were on the ground. This time, though, I just quickly said, "United Flight 26 crashed at 3 a.m." and hung up as we were so busy. They called back and said, "Did you say crashed?" I advised that was correct.

A good friend of mine, Judy Bell, was also on duty that night. There were several hearings in Denver that involved us. When the investigators got through quizzing me, I wasn't even sure I had seen an airplane that night. I don't know the outcome of the hearings, except that the pilot took the entire blame. He said he momentarily looked at the ground, rather than staying with his instruments until final approach. My observation was that he was too low when he broke out of the clouds and should never have tried to come in to Cheyenne that night. There was also some talk of icing on the wings, which could have affected his altitude and controls.

Besides my work, I kept plenty busy with some flight instructing in Laramie on the side. I also enjoyed a lot of car trips into the Snowy Range between Laramie and Rawlings. We found some desolate country and some very beautiful land in southern Wyoming. Marion and I took a few short flights and flew back to Wichita a couple of times. I went to Denver fairly often to visit old friends and always enjoyed seeing the McEnultys again. Mostly I have wonderful memories of those care-free days.

For some reason, I was determined to go home for Christmas in 1946. I had missed one Christmas in 1945 and wanted to be with my family. I asked for the time off and Don said he had already promised Judy she could go home to Missouri. I thought if I worked the midnight shift (11-7) on Christmas Day, I could go home anyway. So I made reservations on Continental for Christmas morning after I got off duty. The day before Christmas I told Don I was going home and he said if I did, I was through. So, I worked my last shift for CAA on December 25, 1946. My Dad thought I was out of my mind to quit such a good job and he was probably right. However, I never had any regrets as the war was over and the men were coming back for these jobs we held while they were gone.

I got a job ferrying a new Cessna 120 from Wichita back to Laramie on January 1, 1947. The snow was quite deep and the temperature in the early morning was minus 18 degrees. Also, there was a lot of ice fog in the air. (Ice fog is a mist that deposits ice crystals on your wings as you fly and can be treacherous.) I went to the Cessna factory to take delivery, but the plane wouldn't start, so they towed it into a hangar to warm it up and dust the snow and ice from its wings. After it started, the snow was too deep to taxi, so they towed me to the end of the runway and I took off in my own tracks.

Bess Streeter, one of my students, went with me as far as Denver. We had no radio and no heater in the plane. We had boots and all sorts of clothes on to keep warm. All the way, we kept our eyes open for a field to land in if the engine quit. All went well and when we got to Denver, the temperature was a toasty 35 degrees. After dropping

Bess off in Denver I flew on to Laramie. By now, it was getting dark and the people in Laramie had given up on me bringing the plane in that night. There was nobody at the field, but somehow I got a way into town. Another lucky trip.

I stayed in Laramie for about three months, hoping to do flight instructing. However, I wasn't well acquainted there and people were skeptical of female instructors at that time so I didn't have enough students to make a go of it. I took a job at Easter time for Woolworth's sacking Easter eggs but didn't last even one day at that job. I don't remember if I fouled up or just didn't want to do that job, but one day was enough. I decided to go back to Wichita in about April of 1947. Marion and I were still dating and there was no trouble between us, but it seemed to be going nowhere. I thought it was time to get out. It was the best move I could have made at that time. Exciting things were in the offing.

UNIVERSITY AIRPORT AT WICHITA

MEETING VAN

I moved back home with the folks again after returning from Cheyenne. They must have thought I would never move out for good; however, there was never a problem that I knew of and it was a lot cheaper than getting an apartment.

Soon after I arrived back in Wichita I went to work at University Airport. This was the former home of Swallow Aircraft at 25th and Hillside on the north side of town. As I understand it, the first airplane that was manufactured commercially in the United States was built at this field. Now, in 1947, Jack Thomas and Eddie Ottaway had a very successful flight school here. Eddie was the one who gave me my first flight lessons in 1938. Many GIs were coming back from the war and could learn to fly on the GI Bill. A lot of fellows took advantage of this opportunity, so there was no shortage of students and the fees were ensured by the government. I was hired as assistant secretary to keep track of students' flight hours and to help schedule the airplanes. I also did some flight instructing and ferry work.

I had a lot of interesting flying experiences at University. I was landing a Cub one day and touched down on a fairly windy day when the landing gear on one side collapsed. A pin had come out but I was landing at such a slow speed that it went down very easily with no damage to the plane. I flew a Fairchild PT19 with an older man who couldn't fly alone any more. We both loved to fly that open-cockpit plane. The airport owned a Seabee, a small amphibian plane. One day

Eddie and I flew over to the Augusta city lake. We were practicing landings on the lake when the police flagged us down and said we couldn't land there as it was a city water supply.

One day, I was checking out a pilot who I knew had a lot of flying time. We were landing to the north and had to pass over a low fence at the south edge of the field. I kept thinking he was a little low, but didn't worry about it as he was an experienced pilot. However, we clipped that fence with the wheels. Fortunately there was no damage and we had a safe landing. I found out after the incident that he had been drinking so wasn't using his best judgment. Had I known that, I would have taken over on the landing.

I almost gave Eddie heart failure one day. He took three of us pilots to Kansas City to ferry three new Stinsons back. The evening before, Eddie had quickly checked me out in a Stinson and I thought I understood all he was telling me. He had told me to switch gas tanks about half way back from Kansas City. We didn't fly back together, so I didn't see the other planes after we left the airport. I very dutifully switched tanks over Emporia, then flew over University Airport to check the wind sock. I was flying north and about a mile east of the airport at about 600 feet. I was preparing to turn for a south landing when suddenly the engine started to sputter.

As I checked the gas tanks, the engine quit. My gas gauge showed I had plenty of fuel but I obviously wasn't going to make it to the airport, so I picked the only field available. It was a very short field but I lined up, gave it full flaps and dropped down, stopping just at the fence adjacent to the cemetery. I sat there puzzled about what had happened.

Eddie quickly drove over to the field imagining his new airplane was cracked up. When he got there, he asked, "What happened?" and I said I didn't know, I had switched tanks over Emporia. He looked and said I hadn't switched tanks, only the indicator. I always thought this was a bad arrangement of instruments, but I should have been paying more attention when I was checked out. I drove back to the airport while Eddie flew the plane off the short field.

A student at the airfield named Evart VanScyoc (pronounced van-SIKE) was a handsome fellow who loved to fly as much as I did.

He had returned from the war and had almost 200 hours of flying time when I met him. He was now taking aerobatic training in a Stearman PT17 and working on his commercial pilot license. After his flying lessons, he would spend a lot of time playing the pin-ball machine in the lobby. We got acquainted and started dating in June.

One little hitch during the time we were dating was when Marion Neary flew in from Laramie to see me. I didn't want to break a date with Van (as he was called by one and all) so I left a note on my folks' front door telling Marion that I had another date. That wasn't very nice of me. I never got to apologize to him as I haven't seen him since. He and his wife live in Idaho and I'm sure he is happily married.

Van was about nine years older than I and had been married before. While he was overseas during the war, his wife (who also was named Mary) decided she didn't want to be married any more. She had become a WASP (Women Army Service Pilots) and later became a controller in the Kansas City tower.

I think we had been out on only a few dates when he asked me to marry him. By this time I was approaching old-maidhood so I snapped up the proposition. My folks and my sister had already fallen in love with him. Maybe the folks thought they would finally get me out of the house. Van had a blue Ford convertible and I had bought a Cessna 120. My fellow workers used to kid us that we got married because I always wanted a convertible and he always wanted an airplane.

Our wedding took place on October 10, 1947. The ceremony was at the Presbyterian Chapel in the evening and the reception was to be at the folks' house. As usual, Dad had planned a project for the house — this time putting a fireplace in the living room— and was working on it at the 11th hour. I think he finished his project late that afternoon. I was running around madly getting the cake and all the other necessities for the reception. On one of these errands I accidentally left with Dad's good hammer on my car and lost it somewhere. Needless to say he was very unhappy with me. However, the wedding came off without a hitch. We managed to hide our car so it didn't get decorated by my brother and took off on our honeymoon to California in the blue convertible.

Our first stop was in Ponca City and we planned to stay in Dallas the second night. However, we failed to realize this was the weekend of the big football game between Oklahoma and Texas and there was not a room to be had in Dallas. So we kept driving west and looking for any room. We finally found a motel in Weatherford, Texas. An older man proudly showed us this room, which had only bare floors and a bed. The bathroom was so small that you had to back into it and could hardly shut the door. However, at this point, we took it. The rest of the trip to California was fantastic. We took the boat to Catalina and I well remember how romantic this ride was. The bands were playing and the ocean breezes were blowing in our faces. Catalina was so quiet and beautiful. No motorized vehicles were allowed on the island.

Geraldine, my sister, and her two children had moved to California and had driven my Mercury out. We sold the blue convertible to her and drove the Mercury on the return trip. When we returned, we settled in Augusta where Van worked for Mobil Oil Company. Since my Dad was born there and my great grandparents settled there in the late 1800s, I felt as if I were moving back home. Grandma had taken us to the cemetery in Augusta many times as we were growing up. All my relatives on the Chance side are buried there and for a long time, I thought that was all there was in that town.

Our first home in Augusta was at 602 School, right across the street from the city building. We paid $30 a month rent for this duplex. Actually, it was a house that had been divided into two sections. Some people had moved out and wanted to sell everything to the new renter. We bought all their possessions, including Christmas decorations, bedding, all the appliances, silverware and dishes so had very little moving to do. We were very comfortable in this house. There wasn't room for the washing machine to be used in the kitchen, so I had to drag it out on the back porch every Monday. As soon as I would get it out there, this sweet little lady next door would always say to me, "Are you washing today?" I wanted to say, "Why else would I drag that machine outdoors?" but I didn't. She meant well.

The whistle for the volunteer firemen was just across the street and made a terrible racket. As soon as it would sound, day or night, we would be off to the fire. My husband never missed a fire. It made life interesting.

Augusta was a bridge-playing town. The Mobil Oil wives would try to outdo each other in entertaining at their bridge luncheons. A couple of ladies offered to teach me to play and I must say they were very patient with me. I still enjoy playing bridge, but will always remember their parties I enjoyed when I first arrived in Augusta and how it helped me to get acquainted. The ladies were also golfers and took me under their wing as I learned to play golf. They invited me to join a social club, the Junior Forum, which I enjoyed for several years. So you see, the social life of this small town wasn't too shabby.

We kept our plane at the Augusta airport, which was adjacent to the golf course and operated by Al and Hazel Guy. Hazel and I were both charter members of the Kansas Chapter of the 99s. This is an organization of licensed women pilots started by Amelia Earhart and is now international in scope. The odd name came from the fact that there were 99 members present at the organizational meeting. The spouses of 99s are known as $49\frac{1}{2}$s. I had become a member-at-large of the 99s in 1941 before the Kansas chapter was organized in 1951. Before this, in 1945, the women pilots in southern Kansas organized the Feminaires. They had no purpose except to take pleasure flights together on Sunday afternoons. Among the flights we took were to Anthony, Eureka (where we enjoyed Skinny McClure's swimming pool), Hutchinson, and several other nearby towns. Augusta hosted one party and some brought their golf clubs. We usually took our husbands or friends with us so we had some pretty large groups on these tours.

FIRST YEARS OF MARRIAGE

After about a year in our first home, we rented a larger house with a basement and an upstairs on the north edge of Augusta. The road wasn't paved so was a muddy mess a lot of the time. The landlord lived next door and was always coming over to check on his house. Also, every time I wanted something, it was on the other floor. But I was thoroughly enjoying our cocker spaniel, Blondie, and not working, for the first time in many years. I felt like Cinderella.

I could not have found a kinder, more considerate husband than Van. He was a jewel who was loved by all who knew him. Our Sunday afternoons were usually spent visiting my folks in Wichita. He also loved to shop for all sorts of gadgets and things to fix the car or the house. He was definitely a fix-it man who loved to tinker. During this period, he started to restore an old Chevy that Dad gave him for Christmas. Then he got into player pianos, then radio and TV repair as the years went by. He was also the fix-it man in the office at the refinery. He kept our cars and airplane in good running condition. He was an accountant at work, but his heart was really into tinkering.

Van's family lived in Kansas City, Kansas, so we went up there several times a year. His father, William, was one of five children, one of whom was his twin brother. His twin was Wellington and they were known as Willy and Welly. They had another brother, Arthur, and two sisters, Myrtle and Winifred. Winifred (Winnie) turned 101 in December 1995; however, her mind is not so sharp now and she does not realize that she made it to the century mark. Van's mother died when he was in his teens. His sister, Nina, and her husband, Ira Easter, had a restaurant in the Santa Fe shops area in Kansas City that was a very busy place when the workers changed shifts. Van's brother, Nyman, had a personality that was very different from Van's. They were never very close, but did keep in touch.

In 1948, I taught Dad to fly off Yingling Field (later Cessna Delivery Center). He soloed and got about 12 hours alone, but he really preferred to be a passenger. After all, he was 50 years old and I thought that was pretty ancient. I flew him out to western Kansas a few times to repair Arnholz trucks that had broken down. Dad's enthusiasm and interest in my flying were part of the reason I kept on with my dreams. I couldn't have had a bigger booster. I think my mom worried some about my flying, but was always willing to go up with me. She was a very patient and trusting person who had watched my dad live through his racing careers and other crazy adventures and seemed to take it in stride.

Our daughter, Betty, was born April 26, 1949. She was about 10 days overdue and I walked and played golf and did everything I could to get her to come into this world. She arrived in her own good time, after I had been in labor over 24 hours. I decided then and there that I wasn't ever going to have another baby. I was in the hospital 10 days, then stayed at my mother's for a week before we came home to Augusta. I still remember how green the fields had become since I left home for the hospital. When we arrived home, they had started paving our street, so we had to come in by way of the muddy back alley.

I don't know if I was a poor mother or whether she had colic, but it seems Betty never slept and I was getting worn out. She was a beautiful little girl and was perfect in every way, except in the sleeping department. However, we weathered her first year. Our 1949 Christmas card pictured Van and me with Betty and Blondie.

In 1949 we bought our first home at 1304 Bobbie Street. It was like heaven to have a house that was on one level. It was only a two-bedroom house with living room, dining room and small kitchen and utility room with detached garage, but it was ours and we loved it. We had lots of friendly neighbors on the block who didn't hesitate to bor-row or loan anything you needed. An apple orchard was across the street, but eventually it was sold and houses popped up. The street there wasn't paved either, so we endured another siege of paving.

When we lived there, Van had three player pianos he was working on at one time; one in the dining room, one in the living room, and the third in the garage. We had a swing set in the front yard, a sand box in the back, and the old Chevy he was restoring in the garage. One day Van had just finished painting a wheel on the car when Betty decided she would add her finishing touch and threw some sand on it. I'm sure she thought she was being helpful, but her dad really didn't appreciate it.

Shortly after Betty was born we decided we couldn't afford both the airplane and children, so we sold the plane. We continued to rent planes from Al and Hazel Guy at the Augusta Airport and found it was cheaper to rent than to own a plane and was a lot less worry when the wind came up. Those strong winds in the Midwest have a way of turning airplanes over, even when they're parked and tied down.

VANSCYOCS IN THE FIFTIES

I was struggling with my on-the-job training for motherhood, but rearing Betty was getting a little easier as she got older. I found it was much easier when she could talk rather than cry. She, of course, was a very smart little girl — sometimes too smart for me. She learned to read and color at a very early age. We mothers often got together with our children to compare their progress. It was the thing to do in Augusta to have a lot of birthday parties. One lady rented a church parlor to have her daughter's first birthday party. What a wild affair with about 25 one-year-olds with presents and cake and ice cream.

When Betty was about a year old, Augusta was hit by a big hail storm early one spring morning. We picked her up out of her crib just before the window above her broke and filled her bed with glass. The hail broke all our north windows as well as badly denting our brand new 1950 Ford. That was our first new car so the damage was rather traumatic. We were thankful though that nobody was hurt.

In July of 1951, Kansas City suffered a huge flood. Van's folks still lived in the Argentine district and his sister, Nina, and her husband still had their restaurant by the railway yards. The floodwaters rose up to the ceiling in Van's dad's house and into the attics of his two rental houses across the street and next door. Van's dad was 71 at this time and had no choice but to fix up those houses. His twin brother came to stay with them while they worked on the houses. Both were carpenters and also fix-it men. We went to Kansas City every weekend all summer to help shovel the mud out of the houses and to remove belongings that had been destroyed. Much of the town was under water and a lot of structures were scraped away and new houses eventually built.

Nina and Ira's restaurant was completely under water and I don't remember that they ever went back in business there. They moved to Clinton, Missouri, where they built a house and raised cattle and hay. Nina is still living on the farm.

Our second daughter, Martha, was born in July, 1952, so I guess I had forgotten my vow to never have another child. Martha had no problems entering this world and seemed to know what it meant to sleep at night. Maybe I learned something from Betty's problems. So now there were four of us. Betty was a lovely little girl with olive skin, brown eyes, and brunette hair. Martha was a beautiful blond with blue-green eyes. We were very happy with our two girls.

As they grew, they became good friends with Janet, Patty, and Steve Singer who lived down on the corner and were about their ages. The five of them were almost inseparable until Mobil Oil transferred the Singers overseas when Betty was about six years old. It was a sad day for the girls and for us too. We had all become good friends. We have lots of movies of this era, with the birthday party we had for Betty's Judy doll, and other birthday parties. A lady named Mrs. Marhankie who lived across the street baby-sat with the girls and she always made an angel food cake with a doll in the middle for their birthdays. They really did love her.

One day while we were living on Bobbie, Van had just left to go back to the refinery after lunch when I heard a loud crash about a block away. Van and our milk man, Charlie, had collided and empty glass milk bottles had toppled from a rack on the top of his truck to the pavement. Nobody was hurt but it was sure a mess. That was in the days when they delivered milk to your house in glass bottles.

I had been a Girl Scout when I was a youngster and thoroughly enjoyed it, so when a friend asked me to become a leader of a Girl Scout troop in 1953, I said I would. She offered to keep the girls on troop meeting day. That was probably a mistake as I stayed in Scouting longer than my girls did.

I tried most of the jobs in Scouting besides having one or two troops. I was at one time or another neighborhood chairman, day camp chairman, cookie chairman, board member, and up to vice-chairman of the board. I can remember the times we had 750 cartons of cookies in the house. One year the weather was frightful when the cookies were delivered. It was snowing and well below zero, but we had to leave the door open for at least an hour while the deliverymen brought in all those cartons. Then the leaders had to come get the cookies and take them out during this same miserable weather. That was when I suggested the cookie sale be held in April.

Martha always tried to keep up with Betty, even though she was three years younger. When Betty took dancing lessons, Martha would try to imitate her. Betty pumped the player pianos and, sitting on a lot of pillows, Martha did too. Betty started piano lessons, and Martha played her little tunes. When Betty started softball, Martha was out trying to keep up. When Betty went to kindergarten, she was always best-rester and got to choose the game of the day. I don't know why she didn't start resting at an earlier age.

This is one place where Martha couldn't keep up when she started to kindergarten. Hard as she would try, she just couldn't be still long enough to be best-rester. One day she came home mad as hops and said, "Just check me out of school. All we do is rest, rest, rest. I just never get to be best-rester." We thought we had a kindergarten drop-out on our hands. After that first rough year, she loved school.

Just before Christmas of 1954, the girls, then two and five years old, received their small pox vaccinations. We had a good Christmas as they were the perfect ages to be excited about their gifts and Santa Claus. In early January, Betty got chicken pox. She was just starting to recover from that when she turned black and blue all over. They ran some blood tests and found her platelets were very low. The doctor told us it might be leukemia and we were scared to death. He told her to take it very easy for about three months. He finally ruled out leukemia and called it ITP (purpura). This seemed to be caused by an allergic reaction to chicken pox.

While we were still worrying about Betty, Martha got chicken pox. She got very little attention as we were more concerned with Betty. Then Martha and I got the mumps just after she recovered from chicken pox. This time they were more worried about me than they were Martha as I was older. Then just as we were getting better, Betty came down with the mumps. We had no sooner recovered from all this than we all, including Van, got the flu. Meantime Betty's platelets gradually came back to normal, but it had been a rough three months.

Television was just coming to Wichita in 1951. Van had bought a Sylvania, which had neon lights around the outside of the picture tube. It was supposed to be easier on your eyes. Just after we bought it, I won a TV at a home show. We sold that one and kept the Sylvania although all you could receive was "snow" from the Oklahoma City station. I can remember watching that snow and hoping for a glimpse of something we could recognize. Within a few weeks, Wichita came on the air and we'd marvel at what we could see, no matter what it was. No choices, just one station.

Van was getting itchy to get a bigger place. It was getting a little crowded with the four of us, our dog Blondie, at least one cat, and three player pianos. We found a house on Sunflower street, just across from Lincoln grade school. It had a double garage, a large kitchen and living room, three bedrooms and one and a half baths. Van had started fixing TVs on the side, so we seldom got our car in the garage. It was just perfect for our needs. This was in 1957 when Martha was in kindergarten and Betty in third grade.

Both the girls had friends in the neighborhood and they all gathered on the school grounds to play. On Palm Sunday in 1959 Betty was trying to high jump on the school grounds by doing the Fosbury flop, which meant she dived over the bar head first and landed in a roll. She landed on her right elbow and walked across the street to tell us. We took one look at it and knew it was broken, so headed for Wesley Hospital in Wichita. The injury required surgery and she was in the hospital 10 days. The elbow healed very well without a cast, leaving only a scar for a memento.

Later that year, we learned much to our surprise that our third child was on the way. We thought we had completed our family, but we were wrong. Gary arrived rather quickly September 12, 1959. Van had always kept me advised of where he could be found in case I had to go to the hospital, except on this day. I knew it was time to go to the hospital and we couldn't locate him. In a short while he came sauntering in and we knew he had not received any of our messages. When we told him it was time, it was like an "I Love Lucy" episode. He

99

started banging down the garage doors, rounding up the girls, getting my suitcase, and other preparations for leaving for a few days. In two hours, Gary arrived and finally we had a handsome new son. The girls were ecstatic about their new brother. Betty was 10 and Martha was seven, so they were all over the neighborhood announcing his birth.

Betty wrote a poem concerning Gary's birth so we used it for a birth announcement. It is as follows:

> I have a baby brother now
> His name is Gary Lewis
> He has dark hair and blue eyes
> But sometimes he gets the blu-es.
> He's just a little fellow
> He weighs six pounds two ounces
> But the way he eats, he'll grow strong
> And have a ball that bounces.

We had had him home only a week when he developed thrush, diarrhea, violent vomiting, and other ailments. We took him back to the hospital, where they put him in isolation and took fluid off his head. It was so hard to have to visit him through a window. They found nothing serious, although they had suspected hydrocephalus, but it took about a year to straighten out his digestive system. Needless to say, he cried a lot and required a lot of care. After that first rough year, we really enjoyed him and he developed very normally until he was about five years old.

In 1960, Betty noticed her left hand was not as big as her right. Sure enough, it had started to atrophy. The doctors sent her to KU Medical center for a diagnosis. They could come up with no explanation except her ulnar nerve was not functioning. The only thing anybody could guess was that when her platelets were so low about five years ago, it cut off the blood supply to that nerve. She lost her ulnar nerve so has no feeling in her little finger and one side of her ring finger and the whole hand is somewhat atrophied and weak. It has gotten no worse or better during the years and she has learned to cope with it. She played clarinet in the band, enjoyed all sports and is an excellent organist.

100

We had no sooner moved to the house on Sunflower, than our beloved Blondie died. We had gotten her in 1947 just after we were married and she died in 1957. We think she got some food poisoning as she had been in good health. We didn't have a dog for a few years, just cats. I really didn't like cats, but everybody else did, so I put up with them. We lost a few with accidents and the girls felt bad, but I never became that attached to them.

Granny, my grandmother Chance, died at age 92 while we lived on Sunflower. Van and I went to Wichita and left the kids with the Applegates, our friends and neighbors, for the night. Martha wrote a theme about how her great grandma died and that she stayed with her friends. She was about eight years old and nonchalantly stated that she slept with Calvin Applegate, who was about five. We still tease her about that.

The girls were starting to show their musical abilities. They were both taking piano and dancing lessons by now. They also took accordion lessons, learned to play band instruments and guitar and were in marching band throughout high school. They learned the organ from Mrs. Bagby. Mr. Tibbets was their band instrument and piano teacher for a while but didn't make them work very hard. During their lessons, he would go to the kitchen and come back and say they did fine. They knew they didn't, but both have used their talents to benefit others. Betty was church organist at the Christian and Methodist churches as a teenager. Martha was 14 when she played for Betty's wedding and has made a career of being a church pianist.

OUR FAMILY IN THE SIXTIES

Mom and Dad had bought the Civic Bowling Alley by now and were doing very well. This was the only bowling alley in Wichita that never had automatic pin setters. Dad had bowled in many leagues since the early '30s and was well acquainted with many pro bowlers, including Steve Nagy and Buzz Fazio. After he bought the Civic, though, he was either too busy to bowl much or he lost interest in it. He started junior bowling in Wichita and was a staunch supporter of it for many years. In 1960 he was named to the Wichita Bowler's Hall of Fame for his involvement in this great program.

When the folks bought the Civic, they knew they might have a problem with Granny as she knew that bowling alleys served beer. They invited her up one Sunday afternoon, when it was illegal to serve beer anyway, and covered everything so she saw nary a sign of beer in the place. They thought they had her convinced when a tattle-tale niece from El Dorado assured her they were selling beer. Mom's solution to the problem was to state that she didn't sell beer; it was there if the customers wanted it. They could help themselves and pay on the honor system. It seemed to work. Geraldine met one of the beer salesmen a few years ago and she told him the story. He said, "For a place that didn't sell beer, I sure delivered a lot up there."

Mom hadn't worked outside the home since they were married, but, as usual, she adjusted to new things very well. She was manager of the coffee counter and did a great job making and selling sandwiches, snacks and pop. She was also on a bowling team for a while. She wasn't very good, but had a lot of fun with the gals on the team.

Dad was not one to be confined too long, so he frequently left her in charge of the entire place. He always said he would be right back, but time wasn't important to him. This was a big source of aggravation to her because the bowling alley was more than she could handle alone but there was no changing his life-long habits. When he was at Arnholz Coffee, she never knew when he would show up for a meal or how many he would bring with him. But that didn't bother her so much then as she had plenty of other things to do at home while waiting for him.

I don't know where Dad got all his crazy ideas, but he pulled one of his famous tricks at the Civic as long as he could get away with it. He had made a bowling ball out of balsa wood, which is very light weight. He drilled the holes and painted it so it looked just like a regular bowling ball. It was so realistic it would fool anybody — until that person picked it up.

Dad's trick was to wait until he heard someone he knew (and was probably expecting) come up the stairs. Then, when the visitor got past the last landing, Dad would throw this ball at him. It would scare him to death, thinking a real ball was hurtling through the air straight at him.

They sold the alleys in the early 1960s and Dad limited his activities to working in the garage he built behind his house restoring old motorcycles and cars. They took a few trips to California and parts west, mostly collecting "choice plunder" and visiting people like Bill Harrah and Floyd Clymer. These were people he had known through his old car and motorcycle interests.

In the meantime my brother, Harold, had established the Chance Manufacturing Company, which produces carousels and other amusement rides. In essence, it began with the roller coaster Dad built as a kid from the top of his family's barn to the street. It went on from there to motorcycles, boats, cars and other vehicles. Harold, who had picked up Dad's mechanical abilities, loved anything to do with transportation and had been a part of our family carnival in Colorado. It was only natural that he would gravitate to that type of business. After his stint in the Army, he went on the road with some carnival rides to various little towns in Kansas and Missouri, but it was lean going.

One time Harold and his carnival crew were headed east out of Augusta in their junky old trucks when the police stopped them and said to follow them back into town. When Harold and the others tried to stop after returning to Augusta, the brakes failed on one of the trucks and it hit the back of the police car. The police immediately impounded the truck. After several days, Harold decided to go pick up the truck — without permission. He never heard from them, so I think the police were glad to get rid of it. This incident probably had a big bearing on Harold wanting to get out of the carnival business.

He then went to work with Herb Ottaway and his family at Joyland, the state's first major amusement park. The Ottaways had been manufacturing trains, one of which Herb Ottaway had taken out to Colorado to team up with our summer carnival. All together the Ottaways manufactured 89 steam trains. They opened a small amusement park on east Central, then opened Joyland in 1949. Harold installed the track for the train ride at Joyland and operated it at a good profit.

Eventually he decided that manufacturing trains and other rides offered a better opportunity, so in 1954, he and the Ottaways made a trade: his train ride for their manufacturing facilities north of town and the little steam train. The business grew under Harold's leadership and, in 1960, moved to its new and expanded location and became Chance Manufacturing Company. Now, as Chance Industries, under the ownership of Harold's son, Dick, they make carousels with beautiful, handpainted animals and a great variety of carnival rides that are sold all over the world. They also manufacture city buses and old-fashioned trolleys. From one train to a huge plant employing more than 400 craftsmen. Truly an American dream.

Back in Augusta, our family of five decided it was time to move again. Van found a very nice house with a huge garage that we called our barn. He thought it would be ideal for his radio and TV repair business. Although he was working full-time at Mobil in the office he was getting quite busy in his spare time fixing TVs so the barn worked out well. He didn't charge much, but he made money with this little side business.

104

The house was across the street from Robinson elementary school so it was handy to live there as Gary was two years old when we moved and the girls were nine and twelve. We were on Lichlyter and Summit streets, but had a hard time spelling Lichlyter, so we changed the address to 415 W. Summit. The house had three bedrooms, a full finished basement, and an intercom system. The yard was lined with beautiful cedar trees and had lots of peach trees and a dandy strawberry patch.

I started doing substitute teaching in physical education about this time while a good friend kept Gary for me. She had a son, also named Gary, and the two boys were about the same age so they had a great time together. The next year I was offered the permanent job of teaching PE on a half-day basis. This was just perfect for me with the responsibilities of home. I taught afternoons for about 12 years. Both the girls eventually had me for their gym teacher. They didn't seem to mind and of course they got A's.

Every year we would all decide where we wanted to go on our next vacation, then save for a year. We had a "vacation can" where we stashed any spare money we made. This way we went to Colorado, Texas, Missouri, South Dakota, Nebraska, and California. Later we took in the eastern and southern states. Those were memorable trips, which we have recorded on slides and movies. We visited Van's sister's farm in Missouri about three times a year where Nina would cook up a storm for us. We always went to Clinton to walk around the town square and to eat lunch, then would take little side trips in the hills. We would only stay a weekend, but we looked forward to these visits. We would go out on the tractor to count the cattle, ride horses, fish, and end the day sitting on the screened-in porch talking and reminiscing. It was so peaceful and pleasant over there.

Betty began to date while she was in high school. She was a very pretty girl, always a good student, played the organ and played the clarinet in the band. Outside school, she took part in church activities and was in Girl Scouts, earning her God and Community Girl Scout Award when she was 15. She started going with Dan Carter, who had just returned to Augusta from the Navy. They went together for about a year and decided to get married after her junior year in school, 1966.

They had a nice church wedding with Martha playing the organ. Betty finished high school in 1967 and their son, Danny, was born in August of that year.

The rest of us had gone to Estes Park for a two-week vacation as Danny wasn't due until September. I warned her not to have him until we got back, but she didn't listen. We were awakened by the landlord at the cabins one night saying we had a phone call. It was Dan telling us that Betty was in the hospital about to have the baby. I don't know what he wanted us to do about it, but I guess he had to talk to somebody. All was well and Danny was a healthy five-pound boy, so we continued our vacation.

One way in which Martha differed from Betty was in her attitude toward boys. She not only wasn't interested in them at an early age but thought most of them were nerds or jerks. She also was a good student, musical, and played the saxophone in the band. She was the accompanist for most of the contestants in various music contests. She and Betty became very good accompanists for a number of musical events in Augusta.

The school system put on two special musical events every year. One was the Christmas program, in which every class from third grade through high school did a number in costume. Then the Bandorama program in the spring showed the progress of the bands from fifth grade through high school. It was spectacular and quite interesting to see how they improved each year.

At a very early age Gary became interested in Match Box cars, which he and his dad collected. He and his friends spent many hours playing with them. He also learned to ride a bicycle on Summit Street. He started to kindergarten in 1964 at Robinson before we were on the move again.

While he was in kindergarten Gary started falling quite a bit and had a lot of trouble getting up. Over the next couple of years he gradually became worse and began walking on his toes and his back started bowing so he could keep his balance. We and his teachers became quite concerned. The local doctor could not figure out his problem so sent us to a doctor in Oklahoma City. This doctor sent us to the Children's Hospital to see a neurologist. Imagine our shock

106

when she told us she wanted Gary and me to go through the research program at the hospital as soon as we could. She was pretty sure he had muscular dystrophy.

Gary had his seventh birthday while we were down there and his prognosis wasn't very bright. We drove home in almost complete silence and shock. Mother called us when we got home to find out about Gary. Then she gave us our second shock. Dad had been taken to the hospital that day with encephalitis and they weren't sure he was going to make it. This delayed our going back to Oklahoma City until Dad's condition improved somewhat.

The stay in Children's Hospital was about the worst I ever experienced. Gary and I shared a small, depressing room in which the windows were boarded up and I had to stoop to get through the door. Apparently another child had had this room and needed it fixed this way for some reason. There were only seven children on the ward and I was the only adult. I couldn't get off the floor unless I was accompanied by a nurse. The TV hardly worked, the kids weren't very well behaved as they all had serious ailments and it rained all the time we were there.

For research purposes I had to go through all the tests Gary did. We both had a muscle biopsy in the calves of our legs. The surgeon's assistant carelessly threw mine in the trash and they frantically hunted for it. Fortunately they found it so we didn't have to do it again. By the middle of the week, I was going stir crazy and kept asking if we could go outside. We finally got outside, only to be driven back by the mosquitoes. Finally, Van and Martha rescued us and we got to go home, even if the diagnosis was definite: it was muscular dystrophy.

When we got home, we limped up to the hospital to see Dad. He was in the hospital a month and was very nice to his friends, but very crabby to his family, which was not like him at all. He made a slow recovery at home but it took a lot out of him. He was fighting to make it to their golden wedding anniversary and he did.

The folks were married over 52 years when Dad died on Valentine's Day in 1969. He spent the day calling all his friends and relatives all over the country. He called me three times, but didn't mention that he wasn't feeling well. When he made his last call about 10 p.m., he lay down on the divan and died. Mom got up the next morning and read the paper, then thought she had better wake him up. That is when she discovered he had died. She immediately took charge by calling their best friends, the Stimpsons, and the ambulance. She was like a rock in this situation.

Not only did Dad die in an unusual fashion, his funeral was unique. Jim Rutherford, his friend as well as his minister, fitted a personality characteristic to each letter of Dad's name. For instance, G was for generosity. Then he told a personal story about Gerald's generosity, then something for E and so on for Dad's entire name. It was the first funeral I ever went to where there was more laughter than tears. Just the way Dad would have liked it. Our entire living room floor was filled with flowers — a great tribute to a wonderful man. I was so lucky to have had him for a father.

Our flying during this period was at a minimum due to time and the expense of it. We flew as passengers with Leroy "Stimp" Stimpson, who owned a Piper Tripacer, which he kept at Wilson Field (now Jabara Airport). In 1969 we started flying out of El Dorado in a Cessna 172 for $10 an hour. This was the first tricycle gear plane we had flown and found it was a lot easier to land than the tail-draggers. It was lots of fun getting back in the air.

In September, 1969, I had a fabulous trip to the national Girl Scout convention in Seattle. I flew co-pilot with Dr. Ward Cole, who owned the Wellington airport and was a Girl Scout board member. His wife and cousin also went on the trip. We flew northwest through Wyoming in his Cessna 182 and ran into a pretty heavy snow shower through that area. We spent the first night at Missoula, Montana, and got to Wennachi, Washington, the next day. Because it was too foggy to land in Seattle, we had some delay getting off the ground the next day. We finally got off about noon and had a beautiful trip through a mountain range east of Seattle. Mt. Rainier and several peaks in Canada loomed large and beautiful on that bright morning. The trip was uneventful but exciting to me as I had never flown over this country. As we neared Seattle, the visibility was lowering but we found Boeing Field without too much trouble.

We spent a week there with Dr. Cole's brother and wife. Besides attending the convention at the site of the old World's Fair, we visited a sawmill, saw boats coming through the locks, went to an opera, saw the harbor lights, and rode a ferry boat. Dr. Cole's cousin Caroline and I flew out of Sea-Tac Airport to Vancouver, BC on a commuter plane. We had tea at an old English hotel and took in the sights of the town, then flew back the same day.

We left this enchanting land and flew back through Pendleton, Oregon, where we visited the Pendleton Woolens Company. Then on to Idaho and Salida, Colorado. We flew in between the mountain peaks — a more spectacular view I have never seen. The next leg was back to Wichita with low clouds and poor visibility. Van and Gary were at the airport in Wichita to greet us. They were tired of baching it.

During the late '60s I taught the basic aviation course at Augusta high school, which added an hour to my day. I was a little disappointed that they put some of the trouble-makers and poorer students in this class. Out of each class of 20, there were only about five who should have been there. This semester-long course was offered for three years. At the end of the class, all the students got to ride as co-pilots and navigators and had to plot their course before the flight. Several students went on to get their private pilot licenses. One became an Air Force officer and flew an equivalent of Air Force One to check the security for the president.

While teaching this course I became active in the Kansas Aviation Teachers Association. Once we flew in a C47 (DC3) to Cape Canaveral where we toured all the facilities. Most impressive were the vertical aerospace building and the huge rocket movers, which moved about one mile per hour. We observed the control center for firing the space craft and saw some of the capsules that they were preparing to go into space. We also got to enjoy the beach for a couple of days. The C47 wasn't the most deluxe plane I had ever been in, but it got us there and back.

Then one windy day, I flew to a convention of aviation teachers in Denver in a V-tail Bonanza. A couple of other teachers were pilot and co-pilot while I was in the back with the president of Sterling College. We had a very strong head wind and the air was quite rough. The V-tail had the characteristic of fish-tailing, which was particularly noticeable in the back seat. I kept telling this man that I was going to get sick and he kept assuring me that I wasn't. I showed him! That was the only time I ever got airsick. The trip back was much better.

The sixties were very exciting times. As you see, there were good and bad times as there are in most lives. As I look back on these days, the good outweighed the bad. We had much to be thankful for. We now had two healthy grandchildren. Paula Carter was born to Betty and Dan on my 50th birthday in 1969. We missed Dad, but were glad Mom was getting along so well. We were learning to cope with Gary's illness by trying to treat him like a normal boy. We were happy to be back flying again.

We also moved again in the '60s. We found the Summit Street house was a little expensive so bought a five-bedroom, tri-level house that needed a lot of repair. We spent the first year getting it in good shape, but Van loved doing that kind of work. We stayed there only about two years when we moved back on Summit, just across the street from our previous house at 415. This address we changed also from Lichlyter to 501 W. Summit. This was our last move in Augusta and I lived there for 15 years.

Some years back, Van had gotten some fire bricks from an old refinery chimney that was torn down. He built an incinerator at one of our houses, but had a lot of bricks left over. He was always going to build another incinerator, but never got around to it. Every time we moved, the bricks had to go too. I finally gave those bricks away at my sale when I moved back to Wichita in 1985 after Van died. I was not going to move them one more time.

THE UPS AND DOWNS OF THE SEVENTIES

The decade of the seventies was a real roller coaster ride with many ups and downs. We were all trying to adjust to the loss of my beloved dad. Mom's first devotion had always been to her husband but now she showed a lot of character as she began doing the things she had wanted to do. She started traveling on tours all over the world. Among the places she visited were the Holy Land, Australia and New Zealand, Hawaii, the fall spectacle of the northeast US, Florida, California, and especially the Scandinavian countries. Norway was her favorite country, partly because that was where her mother was born and partly because it had magnificent scenery.

She brought us souvenirs from all her trips but not a lot of information. She loved to travel and be with people, but seldom told us anything about the landscapes. After she returned from Norway, the "Song of Norway" was showing at the Uptown theater near her house. I don't know how many people she took to that show. I'm sure she saw it at least a dozen times. The scenery was spectacular.

My sister, Geraldine, had moved back to Wichita with her third husband, Al. She had been in California for about 22 years so it was good to have her back. When we were growing up, she and I were not very close as we had such different personalities. I always hung out with Harold and his buddies playing in the neighborhood. Geraldine was interested in the boys and dolls and was much more sophisticated and studious than I was. However, we became very close after her return. We talked to each other nearly every day and she was always there when I needed her.

She divorced Al in the mid-seventies so we took several trips together, but we never tried living together as it would never have worked. We went at a different pace. I hurried around to get things done and she mused on them and did a very thorough job of anything she tried. She was excellent with crewel, crafts, and sewing. She did a great job on genealogy and made picture albums for all our family. She loved working in the garden with her flowers and lawn. Her dedication showed with a beautiful yard. Her slowness and deliberateness would have driven me crazy and I'm sure my whizzing through things would have done the same to her. We both recognized that and remained friends to the end.

David Carter, Betty's third child, was born in 1972. He was a cute little tow-headed boy who was about two years old when he had his curls cut off. Of all the children, he was the "character" and has developed a very dry sense of humor. But things were starting to deteriorate in Betty and Dan's marriage. She and Dan divorced in 1974 and Dan moved to Ft. Worth. Eventually the children moved to Texas with their dad and came to Kansas about three times a year. Betty married again and had two more daughters, Ronda in 1976 and Gina in 1978. Betty and her second husband divorced in 1978 and she raised the girls by herself. Things were rough for her and all of us, but all the kids have remained close through the years.

Martha graduated from Augusta high school in 1970 and went to work in Wichita at Joyland, an amusement park owned by her cousin, Jerry Ottaway. Her job was to run one of the games. She thought Jerry was a hard task-master but was faithful to the job that paid $1.25 an hour. Most of the time she commuted from home, but occasionally stayed with her grandmother (my mom).

In the fall she enrolled at Wichita State University where she majored in music education. She stayed at Grace Wilke dorm that year. The dorm was named after the lady who was dean of women when I was a WU student back in the '30s and '40s. Martha wasn't too thrilled with dorm life after the sheltered life she had led in Augusta, but she stuck it out and it got easier. She attended the University for three years and worked at Joyland for two summers. The last summer she stayed with her grandmother.

During her sophomore year at the University, Martha met Mark Shaw at the Hillside Christian Church where Mark's dad was minister of music and Martha was singing in the choir. Mark loved music as

112

much as Martha did. All the Shaws were singers, but they had no piano players. As Mark tells it, his dad kept pushing him to go with Martha as they needed an accompanist. Martha had never before met anybody she was very interested in, but she knew from the beginning that Mark was the one.

They were married a year later at the church. Danny, six years old, was the ring bearer. Paula was almost four and supposed to be the flower girl, but was too shy to go down the aisle, so Danny went alone. This has been a marriage made in heaven as they have made beautiful music together, literally, for over 20 years. Mark also became a minister of music and Martha has sung and accompanied all that time.

Martha quit college after her marriage, but has never regretted it. Mark and I always joke that he is my favorite son-in-law and I am his favorite mother-in-law. Of course, we each have only one. We do love him. He loves life about as much as anybody I ever knew and lives it to the fullest as a Christian in all his endeavors.

While they were on their way to New Mexico to sing in 1978, Mark and Martha were in a serious automobile accident. In the collision, they both lost their glasses and are nearly blind without them. He knew Martha had on blue jeans and was hunting blindly for her. He found a blue suitcase and started shaking it. Finally he found her and the ambulance took them to a small New Mexico hospital where they found that Martha had a dislocated hip, a concussion and other injuries. Mark had a broken arm and additional minor injuries. Mark was so thrilled that they were not hurt worse that he started singing hymns in the emergency room. The nurses thought he was out of his head, but that is just Mark.

They took about a 100-mile ambulance ride to the Amarillo, Texas, hospital where Martha was put in traction and Mark had his arm set. When I got down there, Mark told me they were going to X-ray his head. I asked why and he said it was because of the way he acted in the first hospital, singing hymns. I was going down the hall while they were setting his arm and heard him singing "Oklahoma!" Later I asked him why he was singing that and he said, "They asked me where I was from." Martha was flown home in a hospital plane in about two weeks and I flew with her as Mark had already gone back to

Wichita. She was in the Wichita hospital another two weeks and recovered for another month at home. They both felt very thankful that their injuries weren't more serious and the damage wasn't permanent.

In 1971 when he was in sixth grade, our son, Gary, went into a wheelchair. We had dreaded that day, but when it came, it was a relief to Gary and made it much easier for him to get around. The kids at school thought it was lots of fun to push him down the corridors. They loved to pop wheelies with him, until the school officials decided it was too dangerous.

Seventh and eighth grades were in a three-story building and his friends carried him up and down the stairs a lot. It was amazing how many teachers had bad backs about this time. However, his math teacher, John Rogers, was faithful to Gary. He was a rather quiet man who never failed to help carry him up the stairs. We are grateful to him and to Gary's classmates for all their help.

We took a lot of trips these last three years. Gary had developed a thing about the Empire State Building and when he would see something big, like Pikes Peak, he would ask if it was bigger than the Empire State Building. We got him a big poster to put in his room, but that didn't stop the question. In 1971, just before he went into a wheel chair, we took a trip through Detroit, Canada, Niagara Falls, and New York City. Martha and Van carried him part way up the Statue of Liberty but the highlight of the trip for him was going to the top of the Empire State Building. Never again did he ask if anything was bigger than this building — now he knew for himself. In Washington, DC, we rode the elevator up the Washington Monument. Van and I especially enjoyed a visit to the Smithsonian's Air and Space Museum.

I had been teaching girls gym in Augusta High School since 1962. However, because of some unhappy changes at the school, and because I needed to give more attention to Gary, I resigned at the end of the 1974 school year.

Gary may have needed more attention, but he still lived life to the fullest. His special pal was a dog named Snoopy, a mixed breed we got in the early '70s. Of the four puppies in the litter, I had suggested one and Van another, but Gary picked Snoopy. And Snoopy turned out to be the best of the litter. She was a good companion for Gary the rest of his life.

Mark Shaw's brother, Marty, was about the same age as Gary and they had become good friends. Marty would get a rope and pull Gary and his wheelchair around the neighborhood with his bicycle. They also made some silly tapes together, such as "Stranded on the Toilet Bowl" with sound effects. On July 4th, 1974, the Shaw and VanScyoc families had a picnic in Augusta's city park. Marty and Gary had a big time at the park shooting off bottle rockets (which were legal then). Those boys had a lot of fun that day and whenever they would get together.

Other trips we took with Gary were to Disneyland and Disney World. On the way to California he lay down spread-eagled at Four Corners with an arm or a leg in each of four states at once and had his picture taken. One of the cutest pictures we have of Gary is after a long day at Disneyland in California. I call it "Tired but Happy." He was a good traveler and got a lot out of each trip. Our last trip with him was in September 1974, to the EAA fly-in at Tallequah, Oklahoma. He and his long-time friend, Marty Hall, got together at the airport, then camped together in our camper. He and Marty got to fly in a Breezy that day. Marty's family practically owned Tallequah and he would point out all his relatives' houses and real estate as they flew at a low altitude in this open-air plane. Van and I wished we could have gone up too.

On November 14, Gary's heart gave out and he died in the Augusta hospital. Marty Hall and his dad came for the funeral, but Marty, being only 15, was so overcome that he could not attend the funeral. The boys had been friends since they were five years old. Gary had always loved drums, so we had a flower arrangement made in that shape for him. It was hard to give him up, but he had been so frustrated because he couldn't do things other kids did and he was feeling so bad, we couldn't ask for him to go on like that. One of the girls in his class, Penny Buell, wrote this poem which was read at his funeral and printed in the 1975 Augusta Junior High annual, which was dedicated to Gary.

When someone is chosen special by God, to live, to
    suffer, to die,
No one has the right to question why.
And when someone goes through life as Gary did, we
    have no self pity to cry.
Then when God decides to end it all, his troubles, his
    pain, his life,
When he's taken from us to live with God, all we can
    say is good-bye.
So now he's left us, but he's better off, I'm sure. Quite
    a bit better than us.
He was courage, more than we'll ever know, a lesson
    to all who knew him.
But now he's gone, believe me, I'll miss him. Probably
    just as much as you.
But we can't ask why. We shouldn't cry. So now all
    we can say is good-bye.

Another poem we have kept on our wall that meant so much to
us after his death is "Heaven's Very Special Child." The author is
unknown but we all found the poem very meaningful and comforting.

A meeting was held quite far from Earth.
"It's time again for another birth,"
Said the angels to the Lord above.
"This special child will need much love.
His progress may seem very slow,
Accomplishments he may not show
And he'll require extra care
From the folks he meets way down there.
He may not run or laugh or play:
His thoughts may seem quite far away,
In many ways he won't adapt,
And he'll be known as handicapped.
So let's be careful where he's sent,
We want his life to be content.
Please, Lord, find parents who
Will do a special job for you.
They will not realize right away

The leading role they're asked to play
But with this child sent from above
Comes stronger faith and richer love.
And soon they'll know the privilege given
In caring for this gift from Heaven,
Their precious charge, so meek and mild
Is Heaven's very special child."

Marty Shaw had a hard time giving up Gary also. Then in July, 1975, Marty was burned in a tragic accident. He had gone to help a friend deliver newspapers early in the morning. They went into a drainage ditch covered with a bridge and found a billfold. They lit a match to examine the billfold and were immediately set on fire. Someone had stolen some gasoline and hid it in the ditch. They went running and screaming to a house and were taken to the hospital. The other boy lived but is terribly scarred. Marty died about a week later. We like to think of the boys as being together again.

In 1976, Mom asked us if we would all go to Terrace Gardens, which was a combination apartment complex/nursing home facility, to see if we liked it. We all showed up and thought it would be a great place for her to move. When we told her we liked it, she said, "That's good, I've already told them I would take it." So within the month, she sold her house, told us to take anything we wanted that she wasn't going to need, sold the rest of the things, and moved. She loved that place and before long was telling everybody how to adjust the furnaces, showing her place to prospective tenants, and organizing card games. She got a one-bedroom apartment and a single bed. That made it pretty obvious that she didn't want overnight company. Once she went to the hospital and I stayed with her the first night home. The next morning she came out and I was on the divan. She said, "You still here?" With that I took the hint and went home.

We had her 80th birthday party at Terrace Gardens in 1979. Geraldine and I had a lot of fun getting ready for that. We made up about 20 scenes from her life with little dolls and other props. Some of them were replicas of the Kirby Castle and the Gordon Bridge; a travel scene with bus, airplane, cars and all sorts of baggage; a doll making

117

an angel food cake and a clock showing midnight; the farm pond with fishermen; a church with people; an antique car with dolls dressed in costumes; and many other scenes from her past. The place was filled with friends and relatives as well as residents from Terrace Gardens.

Van retired after 40 years with Mobil Oil in 1975. We had both looked forward to traveling in our camper trailer. Gary's death had been especially hard on Van. He had really been close to his son and had lifted and carried him with so much love. We went to the Rose Bowl Parade in Pasadena, a first for us, and we were enchanted by the whole thing. We spent two weeks traveling to the sights of the west before returning home.

In May, 1976, Van developed a spot on his lung, which proved to be cancer. We both were optimistic that surgery would take care of it and we would go on with our lives. He had very radical surgery, but they could not remove it all. They broke his ribs and he hurt the rest of his life. Then he had radiation treatments and we had high hopes for that. He was better for a few months, but it returned. He spent the last six weeks of his life in the Augusta hospital. I was allowed to bring my recliner to the hospital as he nearly went crazy when he couldn't find me. Also, he kept trying to get out of bed and we had to watch him very closely so he wouldn't hurt himself. He died March 14, 1977, at the age of 66.

In the last eight years, I had lost all the men in my life who had meant so much to me. Another strange thing was, they had all died on the 14th day of the month. I called upon my faith many times during this period and somehow managed to survive with the help of my friends and family. And I kept busy. Van had been a collector, so it took several months, with Geraldine's help, to clean out the basement and the garage. I had an auction that lasted from morning till night. I was still renting a Cessna 172 from El Dorado Airport now and then so kept up with my flying and other projects.

In 1978 I heard about a job as a juvenile probation officer for Butler County. I had never done anything like that, but I applied and got the job. It was half-time and meant traveling to El Dorado and delivering summonses to people in the southern half of the county. I will never forget the first police report I read. It contained a lot of street language and told it like it was. I guess I had led quite a sheltered life, for I was shocked by the language and happenings on these reports. I did this for about three years and couldn't really see where I had made much difference in the lives of these kids. If they didn't have supportive parents, I couldn't help them.

And that was the roller coaster ride we were on in the '70s.

OFF TO HAWAII

I spent the early eighties adjusting to living alone. I did keep my two youngest granddaughters, Ronda and Gina, quite a bit and spent a lot of time sorting, packing, and selling things that I didn't want any more. Finally I could see the basement floor again and the garage was nearly empty except for my lawn equipment. I decided to take my Social Security at 62 and made more money than when I was working. I still volunteered with Girl Scouts and in the church so was always busy. Geraldine and I got together quite often and we still visited Mother at Terrace Gardens every Sunday. It was becoming rather a carefree and enjoyable lifestyle.

In 1982, Geraldine's daughter, Marilyn, invited us to accompany her and her friend Phyllis to Hawaii. Geraldine and I left Wichita early one August morning, flew to Denver and briefly saw her son Philip, then we were off to Los Angeles. When we arrived at LAX, we found that the terminal where we were to meet Marilyn and Phyllis was being remodeled and there was no place to sit down. On our way back upstairs to a more comfortable waiting area, we inadvertently started to by-pass the security station when a guard shouted, "Stop those women! Where do you think you are going?" We said meekly that we were going back upstairs to sit down. Well, needless to say, we did go through security that time. It was so embarrassing.

We all had lunch, then properly passed through security and proceeded to our boarding zone. We found our flight would be delayed another two and a half hours so found a comfortable lounge to while away the time. We finally took off on a fully-loaded 747. We were scrunched in the middle aisle and had to get up every time anybody wanted out. We were all tired from having arisen in the wee hours of the morning and were even more tired when we arrived about 9 p.m. their time (2 a.m. Wichita time). We were greeted with leis and the driver of a mini-bus who gave us a small tour before taking us to our hotel. We really didn't want a tour at that point, after having been up nearly 24 hours, but we got it anyway.

We enjoyed all the touristy things of Waikiki Beach and Oahu. We went to Pearl Harbor, took a trip around the island by rental car, and enjoyed the beautiful flowers, the beach, and all the shops. We attended a show with a delicious buffet and performance by Rod Tanu. Then we were off to Maui. It was very windy that morning as there was a hurricane brewing near the big island. When we landed, we had to struggle to hold our skirts with one hand and our bags with the other. For the next four days we stayed at Napili Kai, a resort village right on the beach with all sorts of recreational facilities, including miniature golf. We had lunch in an open-air restaurant where the birds flew in and out as we ate.

Dinner at the beautiful Hyatt Regency Hotel with several of Marilyn's and Phyllis' friends was a treat. We also toured the island, went to another Hawaiian show, took a boat trip from one of the hotels, and visited some of the unique shops. I was so impressed with the openness of the hotels. We could never have that in Kansas with our changeable weather.

On our last day in Maui, we decided to brave the "killer waves" then were sorry. I saw a big wave coming so decided to sit down before I was knocked down. Geraldine and I both got caught in the undertow and my knee was pulled backward and the rest of me forward, so I ended up with a torn ligament in my knee. Geraldine was bruised and battered, but her biggest concern was that she would tear holes in her new bathing suit. As it turned out, she was just loaded with sand and was left with a number of bruises but the bathing suit was intact.

By evening, after celebrating Phyllis' birthday at the Maui Moon, my leg was really giving me a lot of pain, so we turned in early. The next day we were off to Kauai where we stayed at the Kauai Surf, another beautiful hotel on the beach. After getting settled in our rooms, I visited the emergency room where we waited several hours before they put an elastic bandage on my knee and told me to stay off it. Needless to say, that was impossible with so many things to do and see. I limped a lot but always managed to keep up.

This island has lots of rain, so has beautiful foliage. The highlight of this trip was our helicopter ride with Jack Harter, who had made over 7,000 flights over Kauai without an accident. We were all outfitted with earphones and Jack began to point out the wonders below us from the time of take-off. Words cannot describe the beauty of this trip. I got to fly in the front seat for a while and was amazed to watch how he could fly up to a mountain crest, hover, then fly right up over it. I was very curious as to how to fly helicopters. It was so different from flying an airplane and I tried to watch what he was doing. He made it look so easy. We all got a Certificate of High Honor for this flight.

We flew back to Honolulu after about four days on the Garden Island. Marilyn and Phyllis flew back to Los Angeles and Geraldine and I were left without a tour director or chauffeur. Actually, we rather enjoyed being on our own. We were so hungry for good old American food one of the first things we did was walk a few blocks until we found a hamburger. It sure tasted good. We spent three glorious days on Waikiki Beach, taking tours, walking to the open-air markets, and doing things at our pace. We took a ride in an outrigger canoe on Geraldine's 64th birthday. Everybody has to row on this trip, so we were out there doing our bit. While we were still on the beach, a helicopter flew over us and dropped thousands of orchids — orchids from heaven.

The next day it was time to fly back to the mainland. We couldn't seem to negotiate airports very well by ourselves as we had another hassle at the Honolulu airport. Due to the early hour, they had very few sky-caps working. We were pulling our own bags through agriculture inspection, then had to get in another line for our seat assignments. We had a snack before leaving the airport as there was no meal served on the plane. Geraldine and I became separated and located each other just before boarding time. This time we were flying on a Western Airlines DC10 and it was filled to capacity also but the flight was uneventful. Much to our surprise, we were greeted at LAX by a uniformed chauffeur holding up the name CHANCE on a sign.

122

He relieved us of our carry-on luggage and helped us into his long, silver Cadillac limo. Boy, did we feel ritzy. Marilyn and Frank took pictures of us as we stepped out of the limousine. We only had time to reload our luggage to the Marrones' car before we were off for their lake house about two hours away.

It was always fun going to the lake as we could swim, ride in the party boat or the speed boat while the younger ones skied, or use the paddle boat. Even just sitting on the balcony and relaxing was enjoyable. Geraldine had another birthday party at the lake, complete with a beautifully decorated cake. I don't know anybody who enjoyed her birthdays more than Geraldine.

We returned to LA in a couple of days where we enjoyed the company of Geraldine's son Mike and his wife (another Marilyn) and their two young children, Shannon and Sean. We enjoyed their pool (everybody in California has a pool). The next day, we made the sojourn to Santa Barbara and to the quaint Danish village of Solvang. They have such cute shops and unusual food. It was now September 4, which would have been Dad's 84th birthday. We would be leaving tomorrow. We felt as if it were midnight and our dream was soon to turn into a pumpkin. However, the memories of that trip are etched in my heart forever.

When we returned to Wichita, I told Betty and her girls Ronda and Gina, who were about four and five years old, all about the trip. They were fascinated by the stories and for a long time kept wanting to go to Hi Wahii. I do hope all of them get to go someday as it is a trip worth dreaming of.

Top left: Mom dressed for the Horseless Carriage Club in the 1940s.

Top right: Wichita University Women's Rifle Team at Booneville, Missouri, 1941.

Middle right: Marian (Tex) Roby and me at the Unser field in Colorado Springs, 1941.

Above: Here I'm in uniform for the Flying Shockers with Mr. Beito, navigation teacher in CPT program, 1940.

Above left: Ford High School, 18 miles east of Dodge City, 1941-42.

Above right: Ford High's English/PE/everything-else teacher on her bike.

Left: "The Three Ms" at the McEnultys: Marge Haynes, Madelyn Brown, Mary Chance, 1943.

Below: Denver Airway Traffic Control Center (ATC), July, 1942. I'm on the B Board.

Left, with Madelyn Pert Brown in 1992 and,
right, Marge Haynes in 1943.

Below: Denver Airway Traffic Control Center. I'm on the
left, then Joyce Mead, Gil Harwell, Madelyn Brown,
Pappy Soper, Verne Ashford, 1942.

Top left: Clowning with Corrine
Schultz, 1944.

Top center: Hutchinson tower, 1946.

Top right: Cheyenne tower, 1946.

Above: Wichita municipal hangar,
with Lloyd McJunkin, 1943. This is
the hangar that I watched burn down
in 1945.

Right: Our wedding picture, 1947.

Van, *above*, and me, *right,* with our Cessna 120 in 1947.

Below: The Feminaires, also in 1947. I'm in the pilot's seat.

The Chance family in 1949. *L-r, back row:* Granny, Harold, Van and Aunt Matt Holmes. *Front:* Marge, Harold's wife, with daughter Susie; Mom holding Betty and me holding Harold and Marge's son, Dick.

Left: Betty as a two-year-old and, at 10, playing the accordion.

Below: Martha at two and with her accordion at age 7.

Above left: The five VanScyocs in 1967: Mary, Van, Betty, Martha, Gary.

Above right: Mom and Dad, 1967.

Above: Mom and her grandson, Dick Chance, in front of a Chance Industries' carousel, 1989.

Left: Our favorite picture of Gary, tired but happy on vacation at age nine.

Above left: Harold, Geraldine and I help Mom celebrate her 80th birthday.

Above: Pre-flight check of the helicopter, 1984. Photo courtesy of the Augusta Daily Gazette.

Left: Flying the B17, 1994.

Below: As a Red Cross driver, 1995. Photo by LuVerne Paine, Red Cross volunteer.

HELICOPTER LESSONS

I had been fascinated with the idea of learning how a helicopter operated ever since that flight in Hawaii. So in the fall of 1983, I was delighted to read a story in the Augusta Gazette about two pilots who had started a helicopter school at Augusta. They were a couple of real characters. John Mapes, from England, was chief instructor. He had been a fireman there, was married and had a young son. His partner, Steve Betts, was from Australia.

Steve was a charming young man who remained rather mysterious. He said he wasn't married and seemed rather afraid to become involved with the gals. He kept telling me about corresponding with some of them by sending his letters to another part of the world to be mailed. He and his mother had parted ways when he joined the Australian Air Force rather than become a doctor, as she had wanted. I used to really chide him about that, but to no avail. He never would tell me how old he was but I guessed he was in his upper 30s or early 40s. I think he got busted from the Australian Air Force for flying his fighter plane through a valley and clipping their only telephone line. Little did he know when he landed that he had part of the tell-tale wires attached to the tail of his plane.

I decided to go out and talk to them about learning. I asked Steve if he thought I was too old at 63 to learn. Of course, he said no but I always wondered what he really thought. As it was rather expensive flying they may have been ready to take on anybody, so I started lessons in November with John as my instructor. The copter was a Viet Nam-era Bell 47G with no coordinated controls. That means the pilot had to work constantly adjusting the throttle and other controls. Later models did not require this constant adjustment.

124

Flying the helicopter was about the hardest thing I ever tried. I think it would have been easier if I had never flown an airplane as many maneuvers were done backwards — that is, opposite to the way one flies an airplane. Also I kept taking my hand off the stick to point out something. That was a big NO NO. Every time I did it, John said that would cost me a dollar. I had many new terms to learn, such as a cyclic (the stick), the collective (control for pitch) and anti-torque pedals (rudder pedals). I flew that thing in my thoughts day and night. We did a lot of flying about 10 feet off the ground as I learned to hover, keep it going straight down a runway, and fly patterns. One of the things I had trouble with was pushing the collective down when I wanted to descend. With an airplane, you just throttled back and it would glide in without pushing a control.

The weather during this winter had been atrocious and many times I would come out to the airport and it was too cold to start the engine. One cold and snowy day in January, 1984, just after my birthday, John said I was ready to solo. I needed a flight physical so I went over to Wichita that morning. I came back and prepared to solo. I called Geraldine and told my neighbor, Clyde Haps, who had been watching me as I practiced. I wasn't that sure I was really going to solo, so didn't tell anybody else. John and I flew about 30 minutes before he got out. Then I was on my own. What a thrill it was to fly alone at the ripe old age of 64! When I came in, Steve greeted me with, "Mary, I can't believe you soloed this in 9.1 hours. It took me 9.4." I think his ego was a little crushed. As all the people who were at the airport gathered around, Steve followed the time-honored ritual for first solo trips: he cut off my shirttail.

I flew solo several times and had about 18 hours in the copter, but fortunately wasn't alone one day when I was practicing patterns. John and I were making our last pattern and were on the crosswind leg at about 400 feet above the ground. Suddenly the bird tilted sharply and we were on our side! John looked at me and then grabbed the controls. He recovered at about 200 feet. We climbed back up to pattern altitude and he said, "You have to fly it *all* the time!" I assured him I had been and didn't know what happened. We came in for the last landing and sat there wondering what went wrong We got out and looked the copter over from top to bottom and could see nothing wrong with it. We talked it over with Steve and were still puzzled.

Not many days later, Steve was taking my two grandsons for a ride. When he took off, the chopper pitched forward and back and then came in for a hard landing. The boys jumped out and Steve took it up again and still had trouble. They then trailered it to Tulsa for an inspection. They found it had a broken stabilizer bar down inside the shaft. It never flew again. Had I been alone when it went on its side, I would have crashed. Actually the craft was in a stall and I knew nothing about recovering from that position. I felt as though I had used up another of my nine lives.

Later John departed for California where he got a job as a fireman. Steve got a job flying for Northwest Airlines and moved to Memphis, Tennessee. Of course, he left no forwarding address, but when I was to have an airline layover in Memphis some time later I wrote to him at the airline office. He did not meet me and the letter was not returned. It would be nice to know what has happened to him, but I doubt if I ever hear from him again.

MOVING TO GEORGETOWN

In the mid-eighties it seemed to be time to move again. I was having a hard time getting any help in maintaining my house. Nobody wanted to even come to give me estimates on repairs or painting. Also, I had no family left in Augusta. Betty lived in Wichita, as did my mother, sister, brother, and granddaughters. Mark and Martha had moved to Oklahoma by this time.

Georgetown Retirement Village in Wichita opened in the summer of 1985 and it was widely advertised on television. Geraldine and I decided to go to an open house one Sunday to check it out. It was a beautiful place that reminded me of the open-air hotels we had seen in Hawaii. All the apartments were on the outside of the building and the apartment doors opened on inside hallways that overlooked atriums throughout the complex. The decor was superb and the dining area was beautiful with their colored tablecloths and other tasteful decorations.

I fell in love with it and was convinced it wasn't that expensive since everything was included in the rent. A complimentary Continental breakfast was served every morning, plus one other meal each day. Laundry and maid service were part of the package besides all the recreational programs offered. It sounded ideal to me so in December of 1985 I moved to Georgetown after selling my house and all the household goods I wouldn't need in an apartment. My apartment had two bedrooms, two bathrooms, living room, dining area, and kitchen and looked out over Clapp Golf Course from the third floor. I could walk out my door and overlook the beautiful main atrium and see the hubbub of activity going on below. The people who lived there at the time were in quite good health and it was advertised as an active retirement village. Of the 200 apartments available, I occupied the 50th, so there were still a lot of empties then.

Some of the activities offered were bridge twice a week, canasta, jigsaw puzzles, bingo, shuffleboard, beautiful walking areas inside and out, and best of all a nice pool room. I had never played much pool, but thoroughly enjoyed the game. We had lots of tournaments. Ronda and Gina stayed with me quite a bit, so they learned to play pool also. They were the darlings of the place. We took several bus trips to places of interest in Kansas, such as Kansas City at Christmas time, Burlington puppet factory, Spring Hill Farm, and a pig farm near Dexter, Kansas. Georgetown entered about two parades a year and I always participated. I also had my bicycle there and rode around the buildings a lot.

I put out a newsletter for about 15 months, which included visitor and health news and silly surveys such as "Do you roll your toilet paper from the top or the bottom of the holder?" Another was, "Do you dust or sweep first?" You would be surprised how much the residents looked forward to that paper. I finally quit it as it was taking up about a week of my time each month.

I also started taking people shopping, buying groceries for them and in general running errands. I decided I was paying a lot of rent when I didn't need any help myself. They were also starting to take in residents who were in very bad health, mentally and physically. In September of 1988, I moved to Southlake Village, an apartment complex in the southwest part of Wichita.

I had looked at a lot of apartments before I found Southlake. Again I fell in love with the beauty of this complex. I rented an apartment on the third floor again, only this time there were no elevators and the stairs were outside. However, my balcony view was right on the lake with fishermen, sail boats, paddle boats, and swimmers galore. They also had a volleyball court in the shallow end of the lake, which my family and I enjoyed, a swimming pool, volleyball court in the sand, tennis courts, and a nice path around the lake for walking.

This place was much less expensive than Georgetown and still had lots of activities, which my kids and I enjoyed. I bought a paddle boat right away and we spent a lot of time on the lake.

As time went by, the grandkids got busy with their own lives so weren't over as often. Also the Canada geese as well as the tame geese made a mess and were quite noisy. There was a lot of partying going on since it was a good place to entertain. I got tired of the steps, not having a washer or dryer, the lack of peace and quiet, and a very uncooperative landlord. I started looking for a duplex on the ground floor. I looked for nearly a year before my realtor told me of a duplex he owned. I looked at it and liked it, but it was still occupied. I finally moved to this duplex on the west side of Wichita in June of 1994. I hope I can stay here a long time. I love the large back yard, no steps to climb, having my own washer and dryer, and the peace and quiet of the neighborhood.

After moving to Wichita, I gradually weaned myself away from Augusta. I first changed my bank, then dropped out of the bridge club I had belonged to since the 1950s as the members were not able to drive to Wichita to play. The last thing I gave up in 1995 was having my taxes done in Augusta. I still do business at the Augusta Credit Union. The gas station we traded with for over 40 years was finally torn down in 1994. I still keep in contact with friends and occasionally play bridge with the old club, still have my church membership in the Augusta Christian Church, but most of my interests are in Wichita.

All my close relatives are buried in Augusta and that is where I will be buried, so I visit the cemetery whenever I am over there. One of my projects while I lived in Augusta was to write down everything that was on every tombstone in both the new and old Elmwood cemeteries. That took about a year but was a very interesting project. A book was published about all the Butler County cemeteries and all my information was in it. For the year's work, I got a copy of the book. Not great pay, but I felt that it was a worthwhile endeavor.

Mom had several surgeries in the '70s and '80s but didn't let it slow her down very long. She had a kidney removed, a mastectomy, a gall bladder operation, then in about 1980 was back in the hospital with a diagnosis of cancer in every bone in her body. Some person in the therapy department told her she would never walk again. She told

129

him that she certainly would, and she never missed a step and had no signs of the cancer in future years. She took a cancer pill the rest of her life, but we will never know if she ever had the bone cancer or if the pill kept it under control or her faith and optimism healed her. Maybe it was a little of each.

In about 1986 Mom accidentally overdosed herself with her medicines. I went to see her about noon one day and she was taking eight pills. "Mom," I said, "that's a lot of pills." She said she took two for this, two for that, etc. I went back that evening and she was doing the same thing and insisted she was supposed to take all of them. By the next day, she was in the hospital very confused. When she got out of the hospital, we tried to fix her pills so she would take them properly, but she said she couldn't stay in the apartment any more and it was time to go to the nursing home section, called the manor. We tried to talk her out of it, but she was determined. Her mind was never as good after that episode and she was correct in moving. We were so lucky that she made the decision to move.

She got a private room in the manor and we decorated it with her pictures and special things so she was quite contented and comfortable. She knew all the nurses and was a delight to be around, so got extra good care. One day we went to visit her and she and Lisa, her favorite nurse, were on the floor laughing their heads off. Lisa said Mom had fallen and she was trying to see if Mom was hurt before helping her up. Another day we came to get her for church and the staff was looking high and low for her teeth. They weren't to be found, so we couldn't take her to church. In a weak moment, Mom confessed, "They didn't fit anyway." We will always believe she flushed them down the stool as they were never found. She got new teeth that never gave her any trouble. Mission accomplished!

Another embarrassing moment happened at Riverlawn Church. By this time her thinking wasn't very clear. She had worn some underpants that were stretched all out of shape. As we were walking down the aisle to leave church, her panties fell to her ankles. She just stepped out of them as I watched in amazement. I quickly reached down and stuffed them in my coat pocket, hoping that nobody else had seen it happen. We had lots of laughs over this incident.

130

When Mom wasn't doing anything else, she was hooking rugs. We all have lots of her beautiful rugs and wall hangings. She also crocheted covers for toilet paper with celluloid dolls in the middle. As long as Mom was able, Geraldine and I went to Riverlawn Church with her, then would go out to eat dinner, then go for a ride. She was so appreciative of all the beauty around her. She celebrated 91 birthdays and enjoyed every one of them.

BALLOON RIDE, COQUINA
AND RED CROSS

My daughter Martha and her husband, Mark, had moved around quite a bit after leaving Haysville Baptist Church, where he was minister of music. They were at Madill, Oklahoma, near Lake Texhoma for about two years. Then they moved to Del City, on the outskirts of Oklahoma City for only six months.

The housing at Del City was about the worst they ever lived in. The water and electrical systems needed constant repair and the floor in their bedroom collapsed when they installed their water bed. That room was never fixed so was unusable. They lived right behind the church and the preacher lived next door. If Mark didn't mow the lawn when the preacher thought he should, the preacher would be on his case. It was not a good situation. Mark's father and mother, the Mercer Shaws, had moved to Florida where he was an evangelist and singer, so he helped get Mark a church job in Ruskin, Florida. So in the fall of 1985, Mark and Martha loaded up a big U-Haul and made the trek to that far-off land and have been there since.

They were in Ruskin several years where Mark was named Man of the Year by the Chamber of Commerce. He organized many community programs that were well received. They have been in Gainesville for the past two years doing part-time church work and working with churches installing sound systems. He is now minister of music and youth at the Parkview Church in Gainesville. Martha has worked for Barnett Banks for seven years and has had very high marks on her evaluations. She tried teaching piano, but did not have the patience to deal with students. Wherever they have gone, Martha has been church pianist and a soloist in the choirs. They are a very talented couple and both love their music. They also play golf and tennis. Mark especially loves golf and had a hole-in-one a few years ago.

Since they moved to Florida, we visit each other about once a year. However, the trip that was most memorable was in the summer of 1987 when Betty and her young daughters flew down with me. Ronda was ten and Gina nine and this was their first airline trip and their first trip to Florida. We landed at Tampa and stayed with Mark and Martha in Ruskin. The girls were entranced with the palm trees and the beautiful weather.

We all went to Disney World where they rode the rides until they were exhausted. In a couple of days, after resting up from Disney, we all went to Coquina Beach on the gulf side of Florida. The Shaws invited some friends who had twin girls about the same age as our girls and a younger son. We found our spot on the beautiful white sands and spent the day in and out of the water, watching the pelicans dive near us and the sea gulls snatching our food if we weren't careful, playing games in the sand, building sand castles, and getting sunburned. What a delightful day that was. The girls said they enjoyed that more than Disney World. At the end of the day, we took a walk on the beach while watching a glorious sunset. This is a day we will never forget.

During our stay with Mark and Martha, we took in the malls in Tampa and Bradenton and all enjoyed playing games such as Rummy Cube, Uno and Farkle. We stayed a week, then flew back through Houston. We could see all the little tiny ships in the gulf as we flew over. The girls enjoyed the meals and snacks served on the trip. It is such fun watching children enjoying something for the first time. We adults seem to take those things for granted. However, I still enjoy the scenery on all my flights, even when we are flying too high to see much detail.

Daughter Betty has worked for the state Social and Rehabilitation Services for about 13 years. Her work has had many rewards and drawbacks, but she has raised two very fine daughters while there. Ronda has beautiful blonde hair and is rather short. Gina has dark hair and is taller, so they don't even look like sisters. They have done their share of arguing, but still stick up for each other. Gina has had stitches a few times but Ronda is the one who gets upset about it. Their personalities are as different as their looks.

Betty's oldest son, Danny, was married to Tifyne Paul in 1989. We all went to Ft. Worth, Texas for the wedding, which took place in Tif's folks' home. It was a very nice affair with the reception taking place right after the wedding. They now have two young sons, Danny Lee and Christopher Paul. The boys were born in 1992 and 1993 and are a handful, but very cute kids.

After moving to Southlake, I found a small Christian Church nearby. Mom was not able to go to Riverlawn Church by 1989, so I attended Faith Christian. I found this a very friendly church for the most part and got quite involved with the activities there. One Sunday, a friend told of an award that someone else had received for driving for Red Cross. It sounded like something I would like to do, so I did a little investigating. Soon I was signed up and went on my first blood delivery with the driver to the northeast and northern parts of the state. We took blood to about 10 hospitals along the way. We started out about five in the morning and were gone about 12 hours.

Next, I tried the Good Neighbor nutrition runs with other drivers, then the local medical runs. I have done all of those runs, but settled in on the medical trips (delivering people to their medical appointments) since 1989. Last year I drove the blood run to Enid, Oklahoma, and back every Friday evening. I did this for about a year and decided it was rather foolish for me to be out there battling the semi trucks, so gave that up.

I don't believe I have ever done a volunteer job I enjoy more than driving for Red Cross. There are times when the passengers are difficult, but for the most part, they are very appreciative of their rides. Also, those who drive (mostly fellows) are lots of fun and very helpful to one another. We have lots of good times and fellowship during the lunch hour, even if the food isn't the best. I have driven an average of two days a week for nearly six years now and hope I can continue for a long time.

One of the highlights of the '80s was my Mother's Day gift from my daughters in 1989: a hot air balloon ride. Betty had researched the pilots of the area to find who would be the safest. She decided on "Smitty" from Andover, who had been an airline captain with lots of overseas duty. I think she made a fine choice. We had to wait until the weather was just right, not too much wind, so it was July before we took the flight. I got the call about four in the afternoon that things were just right. I got busy and rounded up Betty, Ronda, Gina, and Geraldine and met them at the Augusta Airport. Pretty soon Smitty and his wife got there with their balloon rig and the great adventure was under way.

To my surprise, they put all my girls to work as crew members helping to spread out the huge balloon envelope and inflate it. That was quite a process. Betty and I got in the basket while it was still on its side, then Smitty hopped aboard at the last minute. The crew took out in their 4-wheel-drive vehicle to follow us. This day, Smitty decided to practice for a competition he was going to enter to see how many treetops he could clip. We flew very low and yelled at all the people on the ground as we went by. The sheriff thought we were in trouble as we were flying so low, so took out after the chase car. The crew assured them all was OK as we floated northwest. After about an hour, we landed in a field where our crew had indicated for us to land. They gathered up the balloon in the proper manner and we were all off for the Augusta airport for our official ceremony for the flight.

What a thrill it was to fly on this craft. I have experienced many memorable events at the Augusta airport, foremost being my first solo of the helicopter and the balloon flight.

FAMILY EVENTS OF THE NINETIES

The nineties dawned with Mom slowly failing, physically and mentally. She received very good care at Terrace Gardens and never complained. Geraldine and I continued to visit her every Sunday and take her for a ride nearly to the end. We had a birthday party for her in 1990 when she became 91 years old. As usual, the place was full of old friends, relatives, and residents as everybody loved her. By now she was in a wheel chair most of the time. At Thanksgiving in 1990, we all gathered at Geraldine's house. Philip, Geraldine's son, was here from Denver and started joking with Mom and got her to talking. He had one of the greatest visits with her he had ever had. He had her laughing and joking and made her very happy.

Mom died on March 9, 1991 before Geraldine and I could get there. Harold was in the Bahamas, but soon returned. She died very peacefully and I'm sure was happy to join Dad and all the others who had gone before her. She would have been 92 in May, lived a very interesting life and was an inspiration to her family.

Just over a month later, early in the evening of April 26, Betty's birthday, this area suffered the most destructive tornado it has ever experienced. I watched it from my balcony at Southlake Village when it was on the ground in the Haysville area. It continued on a north-easterly path through Oaklawn where Betty and the girls lived. They huddled in their bath tub as they had no basement. Just a block or so south of them about 10 homes were completely destroyed. Almost every home in the area had some damage, as did Betty's. I called her as soon as it passed and they had not had a chance to look outside yet.

I asked if they were all right and they were but their yard was littered with debris that had been picked up and flung out by the winds. They were without utilities for several days.

The tornado remained on the ground as it hit the south end of the Boeing plant before destroying the hospital, apartments, and many other buildings at McConnell Air Force Base. Not content yet, it remained on the ground and destroyed a large number of houses and trees on its path to Andover, where it hit the hardest. It almost completely leveled the trailer park and snuffed out many lives in this area. It continued past Andover along the turnpike where it overturned semi-trucks and more homes before dying out. Over 20 people were killed and many injured and millions of dollars worth of damage was done. What a way to celebrate one's birthday.

Then I lost my beloved sister, Geraldine, on July 10, 1992. She developed lung cancer in the fall of 1991 and optimistically thought she might lick it. She certainly tried. She worked in her garden, stayed in her home, and was independent to the end. About a week before her death, she called me and asked me to come over to help her with her check book. She said she was afraid her brain was going. If this was so, she didn't want to live any longer. I stayed all night with her, but she would not stay in bed. Twice during the night I found her on the floor in front of her china cabinets, as if she were trying to decide who should have different things. By morning, Jerry (her first son) came over to take her to the hospital. They told us it had spread to her brain and offered to give her treatments. We all said NO. She was very peaceful and content that last week and died within a few days. She would have been 74 the next month.

After Mom died, Geraldine was the matriarch of the family. After she died, that put me at the top of the list and that is a little scary. I keep saying I'm too young for that position. I have really missed Geraldine as we were especially close during her illness, but we had talked to each other nearly every evening since she returned from California. We could chit-chat about everything and everybody from our pasts. So many times I will meet a person out of the past and wish I could tell her about it. I guess I was lucky to have had her as long as I did.

Both Mom and Geraldine are buried in Augusta with other family members. Philip played the organ at his mother's funeral. He was especially close to her and it was something he wanted to do for her, hard as it was.

When my long-time controller friend Madelyn Brown Pert and her husband, David, invited me to attend the Indianapolis car races in May of 1993, I jumped at the chance. My mother and dad had been the Perts' guests when Dad was in the pits for Jack McGrath. Brother Harold went nearly every year and his son Dick has been a regular for several years, but I had never attended.

The Perts had purchased penthouse tickets just a little past the finish line, so our seats were perfect. We attended the parade the day before with a group of their friends and had front row seats. On the morning of the races, we drove to an office building nearby where we had an informal breakfast before boarding one of the many buses for the races. They let us out near the stadium where we walked and then climbed the steps to our seats. The crowd was the largest I have ever been a part of and the excitement of the day was overwhelming. Seated directly across the track from us was a large group of French citizens who had flown in on the SST to root for a French driver, then flown to the track by helicopter. I heard their trip cost about $3,000 each.

The ceremonies preceding the races included a parade of the celebrities in the pace cars. Jay Leno and Mary Lou Retton were two whom I remember. Then the national anthem and the releasing of thousands of balloons, then the magic words, "Gentlemen and lady, start your engines!"

The roar of the engines was tremendous for the rest of the race, so we either used sign language or yelled at each other. This was a relatively accident-free race with beautiful weather until the race was over — then the rains came. We boarded our buses and were home within two hours after the end of the race. That evening we watched the award ceremonies on television honoring "Little" Al Unser as the 1993 winner.

My next trip that year started September 24. I flew to Denver, by way of Dallas — right on the way. Geraldine's son, Phil, was at the airport to meet me in his 1987 Thunderbird that had been driven on Sundays by the little old lady from Pasadena. The main reasons for my visit were to attend the opening of the new Denver International Airport, to visit Phil, and to see the aspens in their full glory.

We headed out to the new airport to see the show, which was to start at 10 a.m. The traffic jam was tremendous with over 300,000 cars trying to get there at the same time. We would go a short distance, then sit for a while, then go a way farther. We were gaining on it when they turned us away from the airport and onto a dirt road so we could join the main stream from I-70. They opened the outgoing airport roads to incoming traffic so we had four lanes going into the airport. The few that were going away were driving on the shoulders. We finally got parked about 11:30 (three hours later) and were watching the planes practicing their maneuvers. The airport covers 53 square miles and is ultra modern. However, we all know it was a year and a half late with lots of problems before the airport finally opened.

The air show was tremendous, with precision teams from the US (Thunderbirds), England and Canada. The static displays included home-builts, ultra-lights, helicopters, and military planes. The B2 Stealth Bomber with its guards was there, along with the huge C5 cargo plane, which will carry a semi truck. It was a great day and we got home in only an hour.

The next day was a contrast from the noise of the airport. We drove to the mountains, sometimes on back roads, through Georgetown, Idaho Springs and Central City, enjoying the beautiful golden aspen leaves. Phil knows those mountains like the back of his hand. He fixed pork chops for supper and then entertained me with his great organ music.

On September 28, I was off to Dallas again on my way to Gainesville, Florida, to visit Mark and Martha. After having to battle the airports at Denver, Dallas, and Atlanta, it was so nice to get off at a small airport where you deplane down the steps. Martha met me holding up a sign saying MOM that was made by the girls at the bank where she works. They dared her to hold it up. It was so funny in this tiny airport.

The main trip we took while there was to St. Augustine on the east coast. It is the oldest town in the United States and is very quaint and historic. I just had to stick my toes in the Atlantic Ocean, even though it was quite chilly. The three of us always enjoy playing games in the evening and Martha and I love working puzzles and shopping the malls. Gainesville is the home of the Florida Gators and is known for its many trees. The city has a law that says if you destroy a tree, you must plant another in its place.

I never dated anybody after Van's death until I started seeing Hank. His wife had been a dialysis patient and rode with me in the Red Cross car on a regular basis. He had had a heart attack and went to rehabilitation so I got to know them quite well. His wife died just after Mom, in March, 1991. In July, he asked me out to dinner. Men just can't stand to be alone very long.

As Hank was legally blind I did all the driving. We enjoyed being with each other until his daughter got a little worried that she would lose her daddy and did everything she could to spoil our relationship. In the meantime, we visited other parts of Kansas now and then and, in 1992, flew to California to visit Karen, his other daughter whom I loved.

While in California we also visited Mike and Marilyn DiFilippo (Geraldine's son). One of the first things we did was visit the Aerospace Historical Center in San Diego. Mike was video-taping our visit and the first thing we came to was a jet fighter in the trees outside the entrance. As Mike filmed it, he noted that this plane had been flown there by his Aunt Mary when she couldn't find the runway. A guide showed us through the museum and he told us a lot that the general public does not learn about the museum.

For a while it seemed that my name was on a plaque in the museum. Marilyn had gone to the display of the names of the WASPs and came running back saying, "I found your name." I assured her I had never been in the WASPs and it must have been Van's first wife's name she had seen. Her name was Mary L. VanScyoc and mine was Mary E. When we left, Mike said, "It wasn't too hard to make an E out of an L." I'm sure he didn't do that, but he is crazy enough to try it. I never went back to see.

We also went to visit the Howard Hughes flying boat in Long Beach. It was simply awesome that anything that big could fly even for a few hundred feet. After we left that display, Mike took us by the field where they fly the Goodyear blimp. It was just landing and we got a first-hand view of it. I was amazed at how many people it took to hold it down. Each had his own rope and area. We only wished we could have had a ride in it.

After returning to Wichita, I had a call on my message machine to call a lady named Marguerite Lawrence. She had tracked me down through a mutual friend at Georgetown and wanted to know if I was the one who had flown in the early days of Wichita aviation. I chatted with her about those days and made an appointment to come to the Kansas Aviation Museum, which is housed in the old airport administration building where I had been an air traffic controller. She and her friend, Pat Patterson, were volunteers out there and interested in getting my history. Pat and I had flown out of University Airport a lot in the '40s and he had been up to the tower many times when I worked there. I went out to the museum and they were going to record some of my reminiscences, but the recorder failed to work, so we just renewed old acquaintances. I had never met Marguerite, but we have now become very good friends.

They suggested I give up a day at the Red Cross to come out to the museum as a volunteer. I was a little skeptical, but finally decided to try it for a half a day. I had met Judy Rombold Chandler, the director, and was impressed with what they were doing with the building and the displays they had. They had a long way to go, but had made a lot of progress in the short time they had been there. That first stab at volunteering almost became my last. I was put in the gift shop with a lady who loved to talk about her health. That is a subject I have great aversion to as I grow older and many of my friends have nothing else to talk about. Needless to say, I changed positions and days.

I met many old friends and a lot of other interesting people who wanted to "hangar fly." It was such fun talking about the old days on the field and in the building and taking people through the tower where I used to work. One of the things my friends used to tell visitors was that I was the one who burned down the hangar.

I started out making copies of all the aviation-related newspaper articles on acid-free paper. When I finished that job, Lavon Carter, the volunteer coordinator, taught me how to take care of the artifacts and how to log them in, how to use the computer, and many other office jobs. I started making files for each donation made since the museum opened and putting the donations in the appropriate storage room or exhibit. This took about a year to catch up and to try to log all the new things coming in. I also was called upon to give tours, answer the phone (although I still am not good at that), and work in the gift shop. I spent two days a week out there and didn't think I would ever catch up. Now I am only going one day a week.

I have served on the museum's Wright Brothers Dinner committee for three years and have had the opportunity to meet personalities such as astronaut Joe Engle, Voyager pilot Dick Rutan, dignitaries from the state, Kansas Aviation Hall of Fame honorees, local aviation notables, and many others from all over the world. The volunteers have become one big family with a common goal: to preserve the history of Kansas aviation in the Air Capital of the World.

Also in June, 1992, I attended the 50th anniversary of the Denver Airway Traffic Control Center, which was later moved to Longmont, Colorado. I was the first female hired in that Center in June, 1942, and my friend Madelyn Brown Pert was the third. We were both at Longmont, along with Jean Buck and Marian Russell who came in 1943. Madelyn and I were written up in the Longmont paper. Two of the 12 original controllers who went to work when the Denver center opened in March, 1942, were present.

While we were visiting the center, someone who knew we were from Wichita came over to tell us that Wichita had just abandoned their tower due to bad weather. It was about noon in Denver and I thought things couldn't have been that bad. I didn't give it any more thought as we enjoyed our stay out there, until we were on the way back and turned on the radio in the car. It seems that the west side of Wichita had been hit by the worst hail storm ever. Every north window was gone, roofs gone, all glass signs destroyed, cars destroyed, etc. I could not believe the damage when we returned. I really can't blame the tower personnel for leaving. I'm sure I would have been the first one on the elevator.

I joined SOAP (Society of Airway Pioneers) while at Denver, at the urging of Arnie Price. Lynn Hink, whom I have known through the years, is an active writer for their directory. Then in 1993, I got a letter from Andy Pitas from Arlington, Virginia, who is a volunteer with the Air Traffic Control Association. His mission was to find the first female air traffic controller in the country. I wrote him a letter and gave him all the names and addresses I knew of and told him when I went to work.

Andy told us of the regional meeting in Nashville in the fall of 1993. Madelyn and I decided to go to Nashville, along with her husband, David, and our fellow controller Marian Russell from Wichita. We met Andy and many other controllers. We were amazed at how interested the other controllers were in learning how ATC was back in the early days. We gals were all honored at a luncheon and Andy said it had been impossible to find the first female controller as about 15 of us went to work around the country June 1, 1942.

I had some materials that I thought Andy might be interested in. He was finally getting to eat lunch so I just left them with him. The next day he told me he would like to have an article that I had written about my aviation career and the brochure of the new Denver airport. He said they might publish it in the ATCA Journal. I said he could do with it whatever he wanted, thinking it would never be published.

The day the movers were bringing my furniture into my new duplex and wanting to know where to put everything, the phone rang. It was Andy calling from Virginia. He said my article would be in the June-July issue and they would send me a copy. It so happens there were letters from about four other early-day controllers in the article they titled "Pioneer Female Air Traffic Controllers." It was a nice article, which they had edited but basically not changed. All of us were rather shocked to be called pioneers, but when we stopped to think about it, we were.

The next letter I got from Andy said that the article had won the third place award in the technical writing category for ATCA in 1994 and we were invited to Arlington, Virginia to receive the plaque. Unfortu-nately for me, this was about the time I needed to be in Texas for my granddaughter's wedding, so I was unable to attend. Doris Starr White received the plaque for us. The group decided to put the plaque in the Kansas Aviation Museum, where it is now on display. All this was quite unexpected and appreciated. Andy has done a tremendous job for the gals.

In the spring of 1994, through my association at the museum, I was invited to fly to Sun 'N Fun, a huge air show in Lakeland, Flori-da. Five of us flew down in a Cessna 210. Our trip to Tampa was uneventful except for one period during which air traffic control sent us so high we had to use oxygen. Marty Benham and I stayed in Marguerite Lawrence's tent. Marguerite has attended Sun 'N Fun all 20 years it has been in existence. She is a pilot and active in the Experimental Aircraft Association, OX-5 and 99s. Still active at 78, she is definitely top dog down there. I was glad that Mark and Martha could join us for part of the fun, but wished they could have been there in time to witness the flight of 30 hot air balloons at sunrise. It a sight to behold. Our flight back to Wichita was delayed at Ft. Smith, Arkansas because of a tornado warning and a nasty weather pattern between Ft. Smith and Wichita. We were on the ground about three hours, but had no other weather problems.

Jessie Woods, a long-time friend of Marguerite's, came to Wich-ita after Sun 'N Fun and is a most interesting character. She is a wing-walker from the '20s & '30s who never used a safety harness. She is a delightful, sprightly lady of 85 who walked the wing last at age 82. She has had quite a life, but is so unassuming and very much a lady. Her plane was three hours late getting to Wichita due to bad weather but still she apologized for being late.

When Jessie was in Wichita, she was the toast of the 99s. Dur-ing the meeting they played a song written about her called "Jessie on the Wing." It was a delight to watch her reaction, as she had not heard it before. She also autographed and sold quite a few copies of a book about her called "On the Wing."

Jessie also was guest of honor at an open house at Marguerite's, then honored at an open hangar at Valley Center's airport. Dave Blanton, Jr. gave Marguerite, Jessie, Pat Rank, and me a special ride in his 1928 Curtiss Robin. We buzzed the field going all of 60 miles an hour. I had received my instrument rating in a Robin in 1945, so it was a thrill to fly in one again. I had flown in a restored open-cockpit Travel Air with Dave's father several years ago. Now Dave's son is about to get his license and I hope to fly with him sometime.

One other thrill I got in '94 was a chance to fly the EAA (Experimental Aircraft Association) "Aluminum Overcast." This restored B17 is one of only five still flying. The flight was about an hour long and I logged about 15 minutes in the left seat. Each temporary pilot got a bomber jacket with his or her name on it and a certificate stating he or she had flown it.

The only problem was getting in the thing. Their step-stool hadn't arrived yet and they didn't seem to have a box. They told me to just jump in with their help. Well, when you are 74 and overweight, you don't "just jump." Finally with a box they found in the plane, I climbed in. I was just seated when I heard someone say, "Well, we just had our first casualty." A man had gashed his leg getting in and had to be taken to the hospital for repair. It was a nasty gash and required lots of stitches, but I understand he was back the next day for his ride. We pilots are a hardy bunch.

Just a couple of days after my B17 ride, the family took off for Texas and the wedding of my granddaughter Paula Carter. She was married to Sam Holland in September 1994 in Dallas. She and Sam had been dating for several years while they both obtained their college degrees. Sam is in finance and Paula is a physical therapist. They had a beautiful wedding in a Dallas hotel with Ronda and Gina as bridesmaids and her brother, David, as an usher. They bought their first house just before they married so seem to have it all together.

Grandson David is back in Fort Worth after a four-year hitch in the army, most of which was spent in Germany. He now plans to go to college. Ronda has just graduated from high school and Gina has one more year. Both hope to go to college. Danny and Tif have two boys now and Danny is in the grocery business. Time will tell if Paula and Sam give me any more great-grandchildren.

DELTA FLIGHT 1805

On March 18, 1995, Betty took me to the Wichita airport for a flight to Gainesville to visit Mark and Martha. The weather in Wichita was much like Florida's that day — just perfect. In Atlanta, I changed planes and boarded on time for the hour's flight to Gainesville. The lady in the seat next to me was very nice and friendly. Her son had just received his Navy helicopter wings in Pensacola that day. She and her mother were flying back and her husband drove back. He was to meet them at Gainesville when we arrived that evening at 8:15.

It was just past time for departure when the captain came on the intercom and said they were having some trouble with the left engine and they were going to run it up. They ran it up then we waited a while and he said they were looking things over. In about 10 minutes he announced that the engine had a fuel leak that was not tolerable, so this plane was not going to fly tonight. Soon the baggage was coming off and we were told to go to another gate to get on the replacement plane. Departure time was to be at 8 p.m. We got off the ground at 8:30 and expected to get to Gainesville about 9:15. We had no sooner started descending for Gainesville than the captain turned on the landing lights, which lit up the entire wing and engines. I was sitting by the window just in front of the wing and could see all the clouds rolling over the wing and lightning everywhere. It was raining so hard that it looked like pavement flying by. I had never flown with the lights on, so it seemed quite strange. I didn't know how high we were or what direction we were going. I guess it was none of my business, but I wished I could be in the cockpit to see what was going on.

We made a missed-approach at Gainesville, then the captain announced we were going to circle a while as the airport had had

146

several lightning strikes, one of which knocked out their electricity. We circled for about an hour but that storm decided to stay in one spot. It was an uneasy feeling as he told us we were flying at 3,000 feet and we were never out of the heavy weather. The lights were still on all this time. He did keep us aware of all we needed to know, but it would have helped not to have been a pilot. Finally he said we were going to Jacksonville as we needed fuel. Frankly, I was glad we were going to land somewhere. He kept apologizing and telling us he was a very cautious pilot, for which we were thankful.

We landed at Jacksonville thinking they would bus us back to Gainesville. But that was not their plan. Nothing was open in the airport except the bathrooms. The passengers were hungry and concerned about the people waiting for them. I figured they knew what was going on so didn't fret about that, even though Martha is a born worrier. Pretty soon the captain called us all together and told us we were going to board the plane and taxi out to the end of the runway and wait for the weather to clear in Gainesville. He explained that his main goal was to get us there safely as he was the one riding the "pointy end" of the plane.

We got back on and taxied out and were soon in the air. By now all 40 of us and the flight crew had become bosom buddies. We were still flying through very low clouds, rain and lightning. When we were nearly there he said we had clearance to land. I kept watching the lights I could see on the ground once in a while. Then as we got lower, I saw no lights below us, only over the wing. I said to myself, I do hope there is a runway down there. Shortly, I saw the lights as we passed over the end of the runway. We all yelled and clapped when we touched down. I understand the people waiting for us all did the same thing. It was 12:15, four hours late but safe.

It was the day after St. Patrick's day and I felt like kissing the Blarney Stone, or the Gainesville runway. LUCKY CHANCE. Again.

EPILOGUE

As a young girl, long before I ever thought about becoming a pilot, I had a recurring dream. I would be either walking or roller skating on the sidewalk then would flap my arms and fly about six feet off the ground. I remember how much fun this seemed to be, then I would awaken to find it was only a dream.

But the dream became reality. I was privileged to fly much of my life. I was so fortunate to have had parents who allowed me to pursue my dreams. I was lucky to have married a man who shared my dreams and to have had children who supported me in all endeavors.

I believe that the good Lord must have been looking after me. He kept me safe, from accidents as well as from my own foolishness. He gave me an inheritance of adventurous ancestors and a life rich with love. Yes, lucky Chance, with a lifetime of chances.